Coney Island

Alan Balsam

ISBN: 0999275925
ISBN 13: 9780999275924
Library of Congress Control Number: 2018906614
CityscapeWorks: New York, New York

Back cover photographs: Roman T. Brewka
Cartographer: Jeff King, Mapping Specialists
Cover design and book typesetting: Odyssey Publishing

In Loving Memory of Rose and Philip Isaacs

Contents

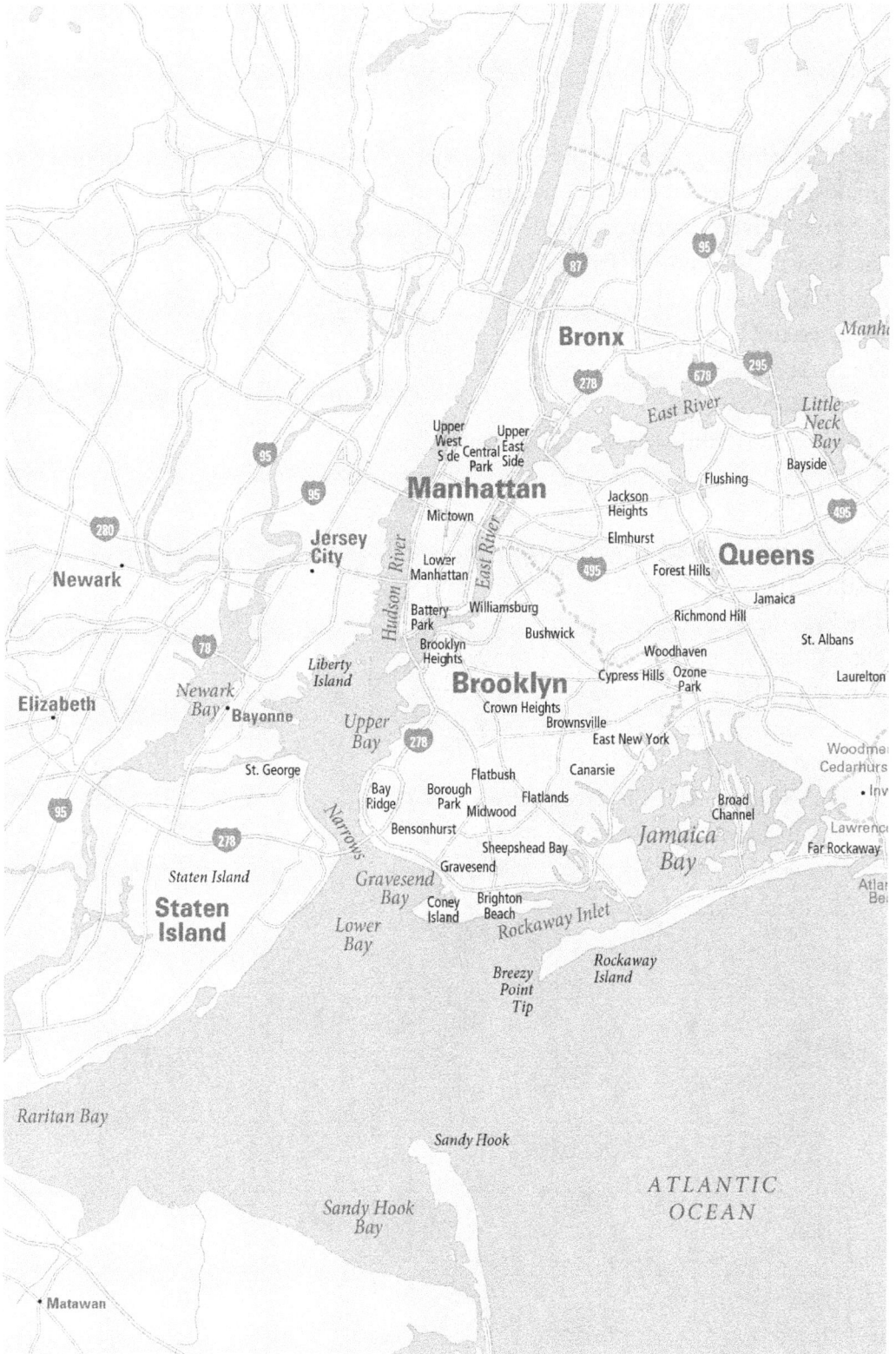

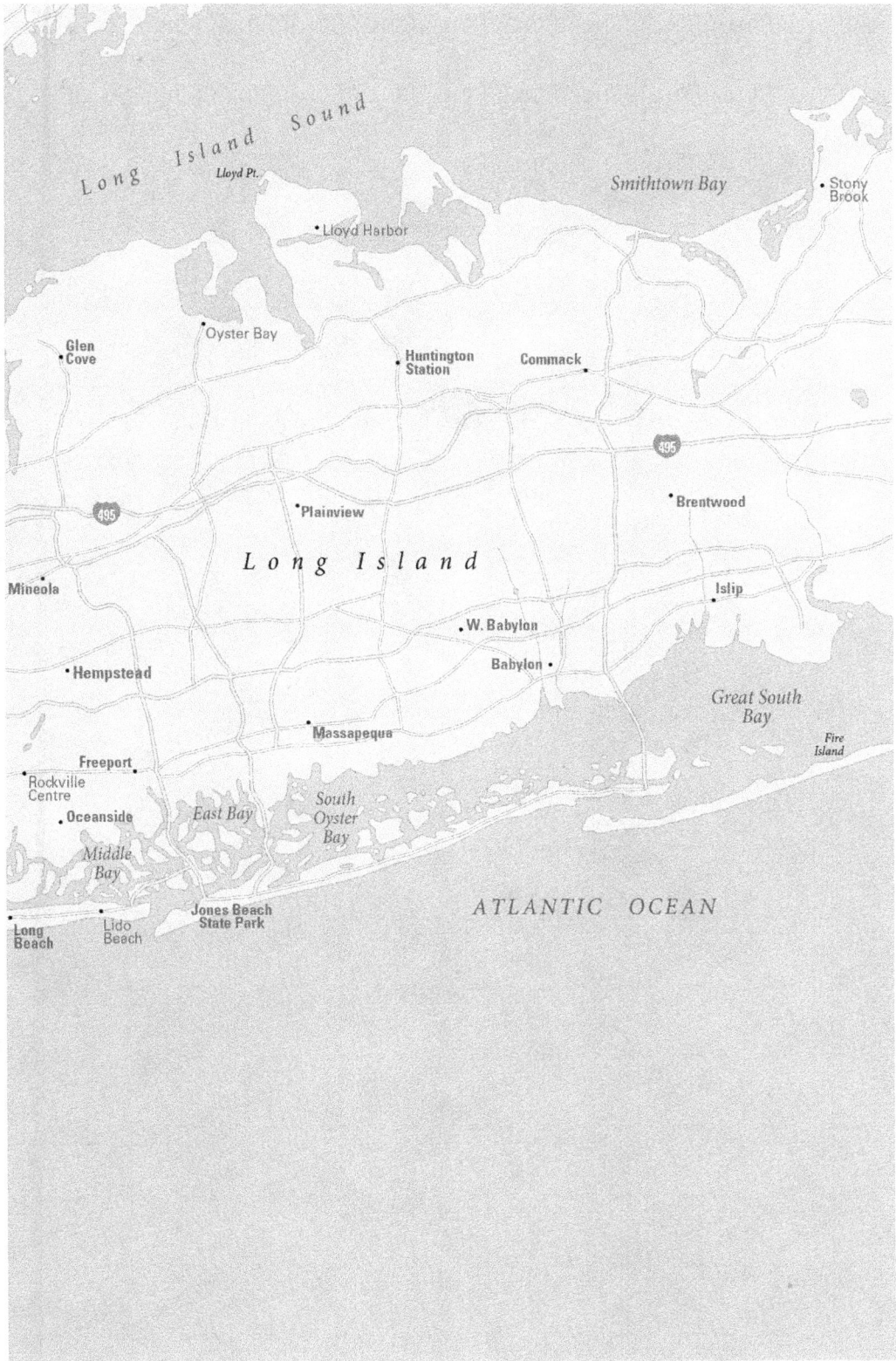

Island of Glory

O, island of dreams,
With shores of hope,
Caressed by winds of change,
Shifting the sands of time.

Island of white sandy beaches
Beyond daily humdrum's reaches
With a legacy of great adventures and glories
And all that history teaches,
Recounted here in diverse stories.

Stalwart sentinel astride the great Atlantic and the Lower Bay,
Shoreline witness to city chronicles of yesterday and today.
Since the beginning of the island's history,
When the mainland was charting its destiny,
Many events still shrouded in mystery.

In early times, development was a remote prospect in its fate,
And over eons the land remained in its natural state,
Covered by thick green forests and traversed by tortuous sparkling rivers
With rocky prominences along the rims of hills of glory.
Daily events likely were very diverse
But there is not much to tell of that story
About the land at the American continent's northeastern edge
Or the island projection into the sea, standing like a great wedge.

Over those lands swallows, hawks, and eagles fly,
Gliding on ocean breezes under a cerulean sky,
And roaming the land were nomadic Indian tribes.
In the absence of historical writings by scholarly scribes,
Little has been recorded of those native bands.
Much of what we know of their ways
Dates back to stories from colonial days,
When the area was in the settlers' hands.

Hunting on the mainland and on the beach sands,
Indian braves rode horses on blankets without saddles
And fished in the great Atlantic, the rivers, streams, and bays
Rowing birch wood canoes with thick tree-hewn paddles.

Island witness to momentous events in history,
The signal voyage of Henry Hudson past the Narrows into Upper Bay,
An incredibly ambitious and heroic foray,
A trip into the unknown leading to Manhattan's discovery,
As well as other places in the New World
Including the shore beaches with unending sands.
The Europeans came when the land was in the Indians' hands
And now over it the flag of our nation is unfurled.
And the first settlement by the Dutch, Fort Amsterdam and the Battery,
Witnessed the English accession to colonial power only forty years later
And in 1776, the bonds of colonialism began crumbling with the arrival of liberty,
A farewell to obeisance and idle flattery,
An assurance of an independent future that would be even greater

And the building and development of the city
By one generation and the next
From strength to strength, in many ways and in varied context,
Offered great hope and limitless opportunity,
And a play unfolded on a stage of history without written text,
Telling a story mindful of the past and things to come next
About a great wave of immigrants from the European continent,
Who came with great hopes and about their prospects for success very confident.

Island wary of the power of the seas,
With no protection from swaying trees,
Visited by hostile forces of nature in various seasons,
Facing looming threats for many reasons,
Appearing so quickly and dramatically,
Exposing its insular vulnerability,
Sending island inhabitants scurrying to safety, sometimes frantically.

The waters have a quixotic temperament:
They could be calm day after day
And then suddenly change in an ominous way,
As dark clouds gather in the firmament,
Heralding the arrival of a tempest from the sea and the sky,
When comes a windless quietude to the area, the calm before the storm;
A brief time of preservation of the scene in its present form.
Shorebirds often linger at that time but not for long,
As the winds indeed will soon become very strong,
And they sense that the risk of a cataclysm is high
And the foreboding change is a signal to depart,
So for safety to higher places they dart.

From where those furies came was often a mystery,
A mostly unsettled matter in the ocean's history,
With winds so strong they would lift the sand to fly,
Creating a haze under an already darkened sky
And furious rains came in sheets from different directions,
Creating havoc on its shore, inundating various sections,
And from their locations on the island even structures would be torn,
Or parts would come loose and become wind-borne
In the midst of the fury of the storm, these accoutrements were shorn,
Leaving the wind-blown, rain-swept isolated sandbar, flooded and forlorn.

At the end of night just before the sun rises,
Solitude reigns over two neighboring worlds:
The domain of dry land and the domain of the sea,
The dark their identity disguises.
Each also enveloped by a mist that unfurleds,
But the end to that stillness is very near,
As the enveloping quiet is about to flee
And through the darkness of night you can soon peer
And see the land of the North American continent nearby, beyond the creek,
A site for a home that people yearning to be free would seek.
Starting at the Brooklyn shore,

A historical truth comes to the fore.
In the stillness of the morn,
When between two worlds people are torn,
Often great opportunity is born—
An important lesson for today, learned from the time of yore,
A teaching of verity for now and evermore.

And over Lower Bay and the great Atlantic
Rises the sun a very great distance away
From beneath the horizon, presenting a spectacular visual display.
Its rays dancing along the endless waters in a carefree antic,
Welcoming the beginning of a new day
As if on stage in a ballet, dancers twirling round and round,
Where only a few moments before darkness was found.
It was as if the night and quiet did conspire
To create a feeling of emptiness, as there had been nary a sight nor sound,
And the early morning sunlight is scarlet, like a blaze of fire
Making the gently shimmering waters glisten
And as the breakers gently roll toward an otherwise motionless shore,
A treeless landscape waits for what the new day has in store,
And all of nature strains to listen
To the music of the sunrise
Always greeted as a welcome surprise.

The first songs are from the gull and plover in motion,
Expatriates from places across the ocean,
Sung while the birds sailed in air over waters so gracefully,
A morning prelude of things yet to be
On the bay facing the endless sea.

Separating the old and new worlds of western civilization,
There is an important geographic and cultural divide.
And here between the ocean and the bay
Comes a truth that is difficult to hide
But rather easy to confide:
The North American continent has been charting its own way
Since the day a group of colonies united into a great nation.

Here, between the ocean and the bay
Borne on sea breezes, swift in flight,
Brought to this timeless sandbar in white,
Are the dreams and deeds of many generations
Coming to this now-empty stage in history,
Soon to be enlivened with drama, pathos, and passion
By actors dressed in nautical costumes of high fashion
Presenting inspiring orations,
From a script with poignant themes and touching story
Which a highly skilled playwright did ably contrive
To be witnessed by an audience yet to arrive.

As the early morning mist clears from the scene,
Yielding to the first rays of the rising sun,
A sandy beach comes into view
Like white satin with a high sheen
And patches of thin grass covered by the morning dew.
After their nocturnal repose, when the day has begun,
And stillness prevails, not a single creature is on the run.

Islands, Bays, Rivers, and the Atlantic Ocean

Coney Island is one of many islands with white sandy beaches
Coursing off the shores to Long Island's easternmost reaches,
Located between the Atlantic and the New York coast,
The joys of which residents can certainly boast.

Popular destinations on any sunny day
For individuals, pairs, groups, or families, one and all
Attracted to the beach by the summer siren's call.
Accessible in all seasons by train and by car,
A breezy, sun-filled place without par,
Good for a long summer vacation or a short stay.

Fire Island, Jones Beach, Long Beach, Rockaway Beach, and Coney Island,
Long and narrow sandbars.
The islands, called barrier islands,
Are near the mainland shore and not far from the highlands.
Busy by day and tranquil under the stars,
Situated from east to west in a linear array,
Tracking alongside the mainland's southern border
And from south to north enclosing a narrow corridor
Between the ocean and the mainland,
Facing a bay on the inland side and the ocean in the opposite way.
In spring showers they are swept by many a rain band,
One followed by another, sometimes for an entire day.

The islands and the bays protect the mainland from the furies of the Atlantic,
From where the storms come from the ocean gigantic,
And the mainland also shelters the islands and the bays,
And it protects them in many other ways,
Its hills a barrier to northern winds, some originating in the arctic,
That blow away the morning mist
And nature's design is nothing if not thorough;
Coney Island itself is nestled under the Brooklyn borough.
Facing south, it is shaped like a clenched fist

With its second and third knuckles pointing to the island and Lower Bay,
It is also protected by another long, narrow island: Rockaway,
Extending from Rockaway Beach to Breezy Point Tip,
And when you arrive there, you are at the end of the trip.

In bay waters stands Staten Island like a massif in the west,
A remote and isolated location thinly settled in the past
But which, in the twentieth century, a stage filled by a full cast.
For a direct route to Coney Island, across the Narrows Bridge is best,
And the northeastern projection of southern New Jersey at Sandy Hook,
A place remote in seafaring days that attracted many a look,
So unique that it merited an entry into the explorers' log book.
From high on the exploring ship's mainmast in the crow's nest
It could be viewed easily with a spyglass; it was the answer to a practical quest.
A tranquil site that could be used for anchorage at the end of the day
In the quiet waters of Sandy Hook Bay.

Bay waters protected by land themselves protect the islands:
To the east is Jamaica Bay, a large circular inland waterway.
For migrating birds, it serves as the ocean's gateway
At the end of a pathway descending from the Woodhaven highlands.
With innumerable unnamed islets in the bay—no exaggeration by any means—
Carved out from southern Brooklyn and Queens
Like an upside-down kettle with Rockaway Island the lid on its mouth
And New York Lower Bay flowing to its south.
To the west and north are Gravesend Bay and the Narrows,
Whose winds bring spring's first starlings and sparrows,
Where eons ago Brooklyn separated from Staten Island at Bay Ridge,
Creating a path to the great North River,
And in winter the mere thought of its northerly destinations makes you shiver,
And where just to the south stands the Verrazano Bridge.

A Natural Habitat for Birds and Creatures of the Sea

The first humans to set foot in Brooklyn, Coney Island, and neighboring places
Were migratory tribes from Northeast Asia, bringing to the area new faces.
They arrived more than ten thousand years ago
And of their arrival there is very little we know.
They lived, travelled and hunted in bands,
And had many distinctive ways,
Adapting to various terrains including lowlands, highlands, rivers, and bays,
Including the islands in the sea with their endless sands
With pristine white beaches where the sanderling plays.
Settling in the areas to the west and the east,
As nomadic peoples they survived on basics, to say the least.

Before humans came, the land was filled with wildlife.
In very early times, dinosaurs roamed the mainland,
The dominant species of the day brought animals strife.
They often travelled in groups, a sight that indeed must have been grand:
Some crawled over the mudflats and swam the ancient bay (the creek) to the island
And moved about on the sand—
Knowing the area, they did not lose their way.

But a general pattern in nature would soon unfold
About which a variety of stories are told:
When one species becomes extinct another gets started,
So, when in the Mesozoic era there was an earthly cataclysm,
Dinosaurs and many large creatures of the sea abruptly departed,
And in animal life there was an unexpected schism.
Burrowing animals, including the rabbit, survived,
And for thousands of years thrived
In numbers that were indeed legion.
Few predators filled the role of assailant,
And so the island was later named Conyne Eylandt
By the Dutch pioneers who settled the mid-Atlantic region.

Today, birds—descendants of dinosaurs—are the most visible wildlife form.
They predominate in tranquil weather or storm,
And visitors from another place
Come and go at their own pace.
When they leave, of their recent visit there is nary a trace,
And according to Biblical legend, pairs of each were on Noah's ark.
An American woodcock comes from Central Park,
A Wilson's snipe from Ocean Parkway,
The short-billed dowitcher and the lesser yellowlegs from Jamaica Bay
And a killdeer from Jones Beach, quite far away.
In the early morning the shorebirds are at the water's edge,
Some having come from a mainland hill's rocky ledge.

Standing quietly, a mixture of shorebirds in a large congregation,
Mostly motionless on the sand, appearing fixed in their station.
It is hard to imagine that they can sing a song,
But come danger they signal that something is wrong.
The breakers roll on to the shore with a foamy top,
One wave followed by another, they never seem to stop.
The water's ebb and the flow seems to capture their attention.
The birds are of various sizes, with long legs for wading
In winds first strengthening then fading.
In the group they stand together and follow convention;
Motionless, on one leg they stand
Firmly planted in the cold wet sand,
An advantage in the wind as it permits slight sway.
As if they came to the beach for sunning,
They hop along on the supporting limb, a very odd display,
But use both legs for any serious running.

The birds stand their ground, not disturbed by the splashing waves of the day
At the moving edge of the bountiful bay.
Occasionally, one or two break rank and run diagonally to higher ground.
They run in the direction of the oncoming waves, a strategy that is sound.
What exactly prompts them to scamper out of the company of the flock

It is difficult to know—it is as if they are commanded by fate's knock,
For oncoming danger is important to heed
As the water makes its way farther up the shore
And strengthening winds prompt the waves to pick up speed.
In attendance are plovers, sanderlings, and oystercatchers galore,
All standing and looking for treasures to be brought by the sea.
Patiently waiting on the sands along the shore,
But then something happens unexpectedly
And in unison they spread their wings
Taking flight, heading for unknown destinations,
Seeking out what the day's fortune brings.
Flocks announce their departure with varied patterns of phonations,
Soaring over the edge of the bay,
Flying in lazy circles, lifted by the breezes of the sea.
In flight, it is much more difficult to tell one from another;
You could easily confuse one bird with its brother,
As they appear so small so high in the sky.
Even at low heights they are a challenge to spy,
As they show a predilection
To turn quickly in another direction.

Sea creatures favor the cold and damp when they emerge from the bay
And are active at the very beginning of the day.
They include an assortment of mollusks, arthropods, and crustaceans,
Each of which the trained eye can find with some patience.
Even tiny creatures with spindly legs, ever so thin
Often not wider than the width of a pin—
They move the most under low light
As shorebirds pose a threat during the day
And it is better to stay out of sight.
So they dig burrows and hide themselves away.

In the early morning hours rise the sounds of an orchestra at the edge of the bay.
The island is the stage and darkness prevails before the new day.
The woodwinds are birds in a nighttime sky
On nocturnal errands in the stealth of darkness they swiftly fly,
Their rapid wing movements are heard in the wind as a twitter,

Coney Island

And as daybreak brings the sun's early morning glitter
The strings are played by the sea breezes, vibrant tones gracing the air
With notes that ascend in a stepwise fashion up a musical stair.
The waves are the brass and their part comes in a spurt
With a booming fanfare capturing attention like a musical alert.
But the conductor of this music is nowhere to be seen,
Though an audience of sea creatures is listening very keen
To the nautical work called "A Seafarer's Delight,"
A symphony with brilliant themes but not a single written page
And the stage is the beach under a star-filled sky in the night.
The performance is a great success, its echoes grand,
And the moon overhead illuminates the stage
With a great white light shining on the sand.

The Coastal Algonquian Tribes

The earliest inhabitants of the region were the Indians,
Peoples who settled in the temperate zone meridians
In the woodlands and on the shores of rivers along the Atlantic coast:
The Algonquians, an alliance of tribes, were united by language, culture, and history.
A nation with great pride in its heritage, of which there was much to boast.
They were known for their strong will and industry.
A peaceful people living a nomadic life, their domain had no specific border.
They emphasized family life and social order
With tribal customs as their unwritten law,
They built family units of brave and squaw.
Encouraging tribal ways and an industrious life,
They did not favor tribal conflict or internecine strife
But defended themselves in any battle
And their spirit no adversary could rattle.
They were people who could survive all the seasons,
And lived by river and wood for practical reasons:
To hunt and fish in the rivers and ocean,
Their spear-arms and arrows in near-constant motion,
And on land they planted maize and wheat,
Which they harvested after the summer's long heat.

Living in harmony with nature's cycle of seasons,
They kept food for when the weather became severe
So the bounty of harvest would last the entire year.
They moved with the fall and spring for many reasons:
For winter they needed a special sturdy dwelling,
For when the snow would come there was no telling,
And they relocated again for better hunting in spring
When the musical birds would return and once again sing.

The New York Algonquians were among the oldest tribes in the nation,
A people with a history of traditions as their reputation.
The Upper Hudson Valley was settled by the Mahicans,
Masters of the hills and mountains, at hunting and trading, they were true beacons

Living in the domain of the eagle and the hawk.
Well-known for beaver trapping and the fur trade,
Bringing their wares to Manhattan and eastern Long Island, all the way to Montauk
On the ancient east-west road at the Terminal Moraine later named the Jamaica Road,
And when they sold their goods for wampum they were paid
And in trading, their business acumen clearly showed.

The Brooklyn and Manhattan tribes belonged to the Lenni Lenape nation,
Who, among the Indian tribes, were treated with great veneration.
Inhabiting the Mid-Atlantic region, they named their land "the Lenapehoking."
They were religious people, the grace of good heavenly spirits invoking.
Their nomadic lives required all the strength they could rally
And they hunted for survival in the mountains and the valley.
As hunters they were masters of archery, carrying their arrows in quivers,
Residing mostly along the North, Delaware, and Susquehanna Rivers.
Some of the tribes lived in large villages of three hundred or more
But most, in small wandering bands of fifty, like those at the shore.

The Lenapehoking extended to the Hudson Valley
Southward to New Jersey, Pennsylvania, and Delaware.
With a shifting population that was difficult to tally
And of the challenges and tribulations
That faced the various Indian nations,
The Lenapes certainly had their share.
They lived modestly throughout the year
And a new season meant a change in lifestyle was near:
In summer, a family lived in a wigwam, in winter, a log cabin dwelling;
They camped in the hills and along the river's edges,
And were adept at scaling the rocky ledges.
They preferred the hills for hunting and the rivers for fishing,
And after the rain and snow led to the water's swelling,
The bounty of fish was beyond anyone's wildest wishing.

The Brooklyn tribe, the Canarsies, lived on the southern shore.
Strong-armed seafarers well acquainted with paddle and oar,
Accustomed to ocean storms that made the waters of the bay roar.
And the Manhattan tribe, the Wappingers, came from the north,

Where the cold mountain zephyrs of winter came forth,
Descendants of the Mahicans, who intermarried with the Lenapes.
Everything was done in groups as it was too dangerous for strays.
The Wappingers and Canarsies spoke Munsee, each with a distinct dialect,
Treating each other as brothers and sisters with deference and respect,
Very different from their relations with Indian nations to the west,
Which were cold and correct at their very best,
Which you might think somewhat surprising,
But there was a conflict reflecting a long history of enmity and friction
With tensions and ill feelings as constant as the morning sun's rising.
Languages and cultures were different and in that contradiction
Lurked many factors that could put the uneasy peace to the test.

The Canarsies visited the island by canoe,
On a route so familiar that with their eyes closed they knew.
At the time there was a bay with mudflats between the island and the mainland;
Coney Island was close by only a short way from the Brooklyn shore.
They went there mostly to fish, hunt, harvest clams, and collect sea shells.
Ordinary shells were used to make trinkets, whistles, and bells.
White and purple shells were used to make wampum, crafted by hand,
Decorative shell jewelry that was also used as currency.
The Canarsies called the island Narrioch, or Shadowless Corner Land,
Bordering on the mainland and the open sea,
A place where the wild grasses and wildflowers blossom
In the home of the rabbit and the possum,
A sight to behold in the sunny wilderness of the sand.

In Western New York lived the Iroquois, a great enemy of the Mahican and Lenape.
The relations between the nations were black and white and many shades of gray.
The warring Indian nations were separated by a mountain barrier:
To the north, the Adirondacks and, to the south, the Catskills,
Periodically attacking the Algonquians in the plains and the hills
On horseback and on foot, each brave a fearless warrior.
With a typical strategy in each battle foray
Built on the insight experience prescribes.
The Iroquois, an alliance of five truculent tribes:
The Seneca, Cayuga, Onondaga, Oneida, and the Mohawk

Occupied an area shaped like a tomahawk,
The handle formed by the first four tribes in the west,
And the blade by the Mohawk in the north—
There was a cauldron of enmity, often simmering and occasionally bursting forth,
Bringing tense relations between the nations to face yet another test.

One hundred years before the arrival of Christopher Columbus in the year 1392,
About two hundred years before the arrival of Henry Hudson and his crew,
The Canarsie Indians thrived along the Brooklyn southern coast,
And it was Coney Island, the gateway to the ocean they loved most.
Children of the tribe were educated in practical skills by a tutor,
A young woman named Whispering Wind.
As a teacher of tribal skills and life, she was an effective troubleshooter
Who would teach the children values and skills to help the tribe in its mission.
Boys were taught practical skills, with no design to turn out a wunderkind:
They learned woodcrafts and hunting, which involved some degree of precision;
And girls were taught domestic skills, including housekeeping and gardening,
And for some of their work their gentle spirits needed hardening.

Whispering Wind had one child, a son named Rising Sun, who at age eleven
Was accustomed to accompanying her on expeditions to the highland.
She would also take the young brave with her on trips to the island,
A custom she had started when he was only age seven.
In summer they would come to the sun-drenched island at sunrise
So as to extend the time they spent there — no surprise —
And they left before noon when the heat of the day turned intense.
In late autumn and in early spring,
When island birds generally take wing,
Cooler weather allowed a longer stay, and before the sunset would commence,
They'd spend most of the day in the place.
When they departed, there was no sign of their recent visit, not even a trace.

She wore her hair braided over her back
And her gatherings she carried in a tightly woven sack
(An early forerunner of what today is called a backpack)
She was clothed in a blouse with half sleeves and an ankle-length skirt,
And wore deerskin moccasins to protect her feet from shells and dirt.

She foraged for shoreline creepers that came in with the tide,
Looking for them in places where they typically hide,
And the luck of the draw was almost always on her side.
The young brave, bare-chested, with a single braid over the neck
Wore a loin cloth and held a hook and line and a bow with arrows
For hunting small animals on the beach and fishing in the sea.
One night, he dreamt that his archery prowess he wanted to check.
He found unexpectedly that he could shoot the arrows all the way to the Narrows
And the prospect of that event occurring while awake he greeted with glee,
Spending the day on the island in the company of cool sea breezes,
Where the isolated visitor over the morning's plans mulls
In a world apart, where quiet prevails on the beach sand
Except for the incessant squealing of the gulls
And the cackling of ducks and geese and many other type of shore bird,
Sounds that were easily heard,
They stood a slight distance apart to avoid tight squeezes,
A possibility they might not consider absurd
In a land filled with wildlife but empty of people
Undisturbed by other tribe members, who were preoccupied on the mainland
By strong winds and cloudbursts that even rendered grazing sheep ill.

On special occasions, celebrations were held on the island bare,
And the entire tribe would travel to that destination with great care.
It was a sandbar in the sea, a remote and desolate place
For a community gathering that featured important ceremonies, usually at night.
On the trip, the tribe disembarked from the Brooklyn shore at twilight.
It was a very clear sky and as darkness descended with a silent grace
The moon rose and cast a brilliant glow on the white sands.
A large campfire was lit and the joy of community filled the air.
There was plenty of noise: boisterous conversation and children's prattles,
Dancing accompanied by music that brought freedom from care,
The sounds from drums and flutes and fifes and rattles
Performed according to tradition by very skilled hands
By the best musicians in the Indian bands.
The dance was a simple performance as well, devoid of pomp:
The braves leaped off the ground and whirled like spinning tops,
Landing, mostly surefooted but sometimes with flops,

Sometimes on one foot and others on both with a thundering stomp,
Dancing in small circles and moving around the campfire bright
And to the audience the braves moved in and out of sight
And their shadows danced under a full moon's beaming light.

As they danced they shouted and sang, it was a sight to behold, one of high drama.
The stage was the open space around the campfire
And in the light of the moon the ocean unfolded in an endless panorama.
The music and singing were enjoyed by all, and few would tire;
The women gathered in a circle, performing the Dance of the Turtle,
 Waving small leafy branches from a mainland myrtle.

The chief and the council were dressed for the occasion in official regalia
And to highlight the festivity the women brought bouquets of red azalea.
The shaman offered a familiar prayer
Which the tribe was happy to share
Near the domain of the sea hare,
Recited in plaintive murmurings to banish evil spirits in the shadows
To a distant place for a lengthy repose,
With certain vocal renderings with trills
Sometimes accompanied by music
Consistent with the ceremonial rubric,
And to distance any lurking ills,
For the occasion he wore special clothes:
A headdress with projecting feathers and a fur shoulder cape
And he looked in the shadows much like a small ape,
Dressed in an apron-like tunic with braided frills
And matching leggings under the tunic.
He waved an incense burner to and fro
In a rhythmic pattern both deliberate and slow.
It issued forth the pleasant aroma of a plant used by the entire Indian nation
And stories were told to the children about events of yore
Alongside histories that had occurred on that very shore
And one they regarded with great awe: the epic of the creation.

Henry Hudson and the Halve Maen

In considering the story of a particular place,
Like Coney Island, an island of dreams and grace,
We consider its promise to future generations
For people of all backgrounds, creeds, and stations.
We also note events in the immediate surrounding
Which were important in creating the dream
And whose fulfillment brought great esteem.
So, we now turn to a time when the waters had their first sounding
On an auspicious visit which opened a New World, indeed,
One to which history certainly paid heed,
Signaling dramatic changes about to come bounding.

In history, there are many instances of searching for one thing and finding another,
A happening usually unrelated to the breadth of the area the search has to cover.
Ironically, sometimes an item sought is less important than the one discovered.
In the early 1600s, Europe's colonial powers prospered
Largely because new places of trade were uncovered;
Most involved transport to and from the Far East,
But the cost of the shipping was expensive, to say the least,
As the route was circuitous, around the southern tip of Africa, Cape Horn,
But when voyage did end, the captain and the crew felt somewhat forlorn
As the effort was great and their return would be extended
And all concerned wished that somehow the route could be amended.

As merchants and mariners, the Dutch of the House of Orange were very astute.
Influential, powerful, and known worldwide, the Dutch needed no introduction—
They excelled in trade and in every aspect of industrial production.
They were determined to find an entry to the Far East via a northern route
And that was the original mission of the navigator and explorer, Henry Hudson.
Sponsored by Dutch East India Company, he was to find an eastward way,
A so-called European Northeast Passage, to the orient and Cathay.

He was outfitted a ship, a triple-masted carrack,
And there was hardly any feature the vessel did lack.

A Dutch wonder of the seas of the day,
Built by master ship builders, of strong wood it was hewn.
Well-crafted in every way,
A vessel worthy of any ocean or bay,
It was named Halve Maen
And had a wide and high stern and a drooping narrow bow
Its broad sails caught the wind and propelled it forward
And it would begin its voyage very soon
As early as possible in the forenoon.
It had an able crew with much experience and know-how
That could handle any nautical events untoward
Like storms at sea that would make the ship swoon.

She began her voyage at the beginning of summer
Without ceremonial departure or cheering host,
Without a fanfare from fifer, bugler, or drummer,
Headed northward in Europe, tracking the coast,
But she was waylaid by icebergs on the subpolar route
And the possibility of finding a path was moot,
So the captain turned and headed west,
A plan of action that he deemed the best,
As he believed there was another route in the northwest,
And that change in plans was entirely his own,
That decision put his determination to the test:
A decision that was applauded by history as was clearly shown.

He headed west and arrived at the island of Nova Scotia
With as little understanding of the coastal lands as of the wilds of Cappadocia
Travelling down the east coast there was no opportunity he spurned
To find a point of inland entry that would lead to a passage in the subpolar zone
And in doing so he left no stone unturned,
Always maintaining proper demeanor and an optimistic tone
He sailed as far as Virginia and then turned north
Into the great Delaware River as he thought his search might be done,
But the river meandered hither and yon and land was blocking the way
So in looking for a passage, he realized that the Delaware was not one,
And so the trip was rather short back and forth,

And that digression unfortunately did not succeed,
But he was born to a very strong-willed and persistent breed
So ventured further, sailing back up the coast to the Sandy Hook of today.

His voyage to the New World was described in a remarkable document,
Distinguished by its importance and historical content:
A detailed journal kept by Robert Juet, a ship's mate,
With daily entries on the voyage, including every encounter and event
And that writing was a great fortune of fate
As the absence of written chronicles we would not have to lament.

The vessel moved northward, and as the morning mist cleared,
With a light wind at its stern, the ship took a straight path and never once veered.
From the crow's nest, Coney Island and southern Brooklyn were easily seen,
But coastal islands were not a matter of great interest to Hudson in that scene.
It was a northwest passage he was seeking,
It was about that he was continually speaking,
And the great North River, now named after him, had not yet come into view.
It was so close, and would take him so far, on the journey to discover something new.

On September third, 1609, the Halve Maen approached Manhattan Harbor
It was a day for work, not for sitting under an arbor.
On that day, an entry was made in the ship's log
About a sighting near the estuary, after the clearing of the fog:
"At three of the clocke in the after-noone, wee came to three great rivers," he wrote.
That would include the great North River, the East River and the river to Newark Bay.
A voyage up the North River was planned after depth soundings from a boat.

Meanwhile, Wappinger scouts in Manhattan and New Jersey noted something amiss:
They spied a large object floating in the middle of Upper Bay,
A sight never seen before, as mysterious as an apparition,
Looming in waters so close to their encampments, a threat to tribal bliss.
Ominous and foreboding it appeared, threatening danger and perdition
And the view from any high place on the shore their fear did not allay.
They reported their sighting to the chief, who took it under consideration.
He convoked a council of elders, in the tradition of the Algonquian nation.

The scouts suggested that the vessel they saw was a gigantic sea monster,
Poised to launch an attack that could be devastating and brief,
But this seemed unlikely to the sagacious chief,
As there had been little movement of the floating object that day,
Only a curious side-to-side sway,
The vessel being at anchor in Upper Bay
On the opposite shore (where exactly it is hard to say).
He said that the scout's explanation likely was wrong,
Rejecting the notion of a gigantic sea creature.
The chief said it was the floating palace of the Great Spirit Kishelemukong,
And suggested that as it came closer they examine it feature by feature.

The next day, tribal people were out in full force.
As a matter of prudence, of course,
The vessel moved upriver, drawing close to Manhattan Island's southern tip,
And standing on hills, braves scoured the approaching marvel in search of clues,
Some still feeling the effects of the previous night's medicinal brews.
A great enigma it indeed was, that slowly sailing ship.
In the North River to greet it there was an orderly display of canoes.
The air was filled with awe and much curiosity:
Wappinger braves and squaws approached with no sign of animosity.
The Indians who came aboard were happy to greet the visiting crew:
They were people of a different background and great respect was due.
They gave them a brotherhood and peace sign,
Their right arms stretched out over their chests,
And behaved very civilly in the presence of the guests,
Offering for the occasion a polite welcome and gifts of excellent design.

The locals appeared well-dressed in loose deerskin clothes,
Wearing necklaces bearing copper charm pendants and belts with wampum buckles.
And for footwear they wore moccasins without hose.
They gave the crew green tobacco, knives, and beads,
And the women brought hemp and baskets made from reeds
And nectar extracted from local honeysuckles.
As individuals who labored to craft family dress mostly without a hem,
They were attracted to European clothes and were interested in acquiring them.

A visit of the crew to the mainland revealed the area's elevation,
A wonder of nature's creation
With great tall oaks and lush grassy meadows.
The American northeastern oak, a statuesque titan
Whose grandeur any forest would brighten.
In the woodlands, smaller trees stood in its shadow
Among hardwood trees it has no rival:
A fierce competitor in nature's battle for survival.

The natives lived in huts with dome-shaped tops called wigwams—
A very compact dwelling whose length was limited to several outstretched arms—
Or in winter in multifamily dwellings, houses made of logs
Built each year with that season's arrival.
These offered more protection from the cold and the dampness of bogs,
And the local inhabitants had all the basics for survival.
Their livelihood depended on farming and hunting for the tribe and the family brood,
And they lived a communal life and shared resources, including food.

The tribe had a great store of maize and Indian wheat,
Which they had harvested after the summer heat
And from which they made good bread.
Among the crew members it was said
That the Indian foods were well-prepared and tasty,
Unlike the ship's food, which was minimal and hasty.

There was a formal visit paid by Henry Hudson to the Wappinger chief,
A momentous occasion in history, though ever so brief.
The ship's master was dressed in his finest clothes, in white shirt and bright red coat,
A popular color combination that the English gentry did promote.
The natives were very impressed by his attire
Which, indeed, was meant to inspire,
But his and the crew's pale skin attracted the most attention at the visit's start,
So different from their own, sun-exposed, with a reddish hue in the face—
By comparison, the Europeans had a definite pallor.
It was as if they came from a sunless place and sat all day in the parlor.
For the natives, it was like receiving visitors from a world apart
And indeed, the cities of Europe were a very different place.

The meeting was celebrated with Indian pomp and ceremony.
In the presence of the chief and the elders of the band
The peace pipe was passed from hand to hand,
A tradition in honor of guests that was customary.
There was also celebratory dancing and singing,
With musical accompaniment in the still of night ringing
And for at least a moment in time.
In the setting of the late summer clime
All suspicion and fear were cast aside.
The warmth of celebration that setting permeated
With its centerpiece Indian pride
And a bond of friendship and peace was created
Between host and guest.
It was an English bond that time would repeatedly test.

On September sixth 1609, a boat was sent to explore a northern area of the river
To obtain depth readings as the water was shallow near the estuary.
The plan was to obtain that information and then to the ship's master deliver,
But a warrior band, unacquainted with the visitors and of intruders wary
Sighted the expedition from a nearby promontory,
And were greatly alarmed by the proximity of the boat to their shore,
And not knowing anything about the visitors or what was in store
The Indians considered them interlopers and a genuine threat
(For of the meetings between the crew and the Indians they had no knowledge yet,
When the chief and tribesman by Hudson were charmed
in his glowing white shirt and long red coat).
They sent a war party of two canoes that were heavily armed,
Men with one arm on the oar and the other on the quiver,
As they glided with stealth down the river.
A shower of arrows was launched at the boat
And one man, John Colman, was felled by an arrow lodged in the neck,
And several others were wounded and adding to the gravity of their plight.
In the dark of night, the boat had difficulty finding the ship during their flight,
And nothing was known up on the ship's deck.
Then the sky opened up with a torrent of rain
Creating extra burden of stress and strain
And care for the wounded was delayed the whole night,

So on the following morning they returned to the ship.
That was the only hostility they met; peace reigned for the rest of their trip.

The rest of the story of the Halve Maen has been recounted extensively:
Hudson and his crew made it up the North River as far as Albany,
Where they learned about the beaver trade in the Hudson Valley
And that the trading Mahicans to peaceful relations were prone
And they were industrious workers of their trade, as was well known.
The news he brought to the Dutch received a resounding cheer
As the favorable implications for the future were very clear—
The prospect of trade created in Europe a business sensation
And the area was a magnet for Dutch settlement creation
And the trade was successful beyond their wildest dreams;
The traders, so different in background, surprisingly formed good business teams.

Homage to Henry Hudson

History often unfolds in an uneven way
According to its own mind, you might say,
And that understanding makes any observer wiser.
It comes in fits and starts, like the first puffs of steam rising from a geyser,
Followed by the powerful fountain jet that bursts into the air,
Propelled toward the heavens with the strength of a fervent prayer,
Hovering like a blue veil, swirling in a spiral dance,
As if signaling the coming of some important chance.

A discovery may occur which things to come presages
And the expectation is for those things to come soon, or in stages,
But then nothing happens for decades or more.
Long forgotten, meaning fades, as with so many things of yore,
But then the original finding, in history pent up all the while,
(And in the intervening time there are many changes in style)
Very suddenly reappears in a manner bold,
Gushing forth like a geyser, and the new trend takes hold.
With newness and unfamiliarity sometimes come fears,
Which gradually are dispelled with the passage of years.
The new is often ushered in with a panoply of parades,
But the novelty of the discovery soon thereafter fades.

People may be considered agents of destiny,
A role assigned to them in history.
They become movers of important events
On voyages with unknown portents
Exploring uncharted seas and unexplored territories,
About which later chronicles will relate their particular stories.

According to the purposeful theory of history evolving,
Mankind shows a positive attitude based on problem solving.
Its unfolding is based on yearnings, dreams, and positive sentiments
A process geared toward new developments.
As humankind strives to improve society for the common good:

A practice that follows a pattern it certainly should.
A person is often given a specific role in history
According to the dictates of destiny
And generally the person is totally unaware of their own potential,
Sometimes leading to a discovery that for the future is essential—
Such was the discovery of Manhattan and the Hudson Valley,
So important was the journey it merits remembrance day with a parade and a rally
To honor the master navigator Henry Hudson and his crew
With all the details we know of their story,
The discovery may be viewed as of that category:
One that would lead to a massive migration
Of people from the old world to the new;
One that was very important in the building of our nation.

O, intrepid wayfarer of the seas,
Indomitable spirit, unyielding to the dark winds of despair,
Explorer of the northeastern American landmass,
A man with a vision and of great quality and class
Who sailed far beyond the coastal sands
Up the great North River to the interior lands.
Heading north past Manhattan and the Palisades,
Covered by the lush growth of the glades
Into the great Hudson Valley,
All the way to Beverwijck, today Albany,
Where no European had ever been seen.
To them it was a place with forests of very deep green
Reminiscent of a landscape that was European.

It was a voyage of the stranger, a mariner into uncharted seas,
From the realm of the known into the realm of the unknown
In a worthy vessel that was tossed and blown
On a trip that was with danger fraught
As in harm's way you could easily get caught.
Reaching undiscovered sandy islands and land with hardwood trees,
He engaged the Native American population
And was received as an honored guest in their nation.
To Europe, he brought back news of the beaver trade

And that became a great sensation,
Prompting European peoples' westward migration.
And once the idea took hold, it happened in less than a decade,
And settlements by the Dutch in the Mid-Atlantic coastal region
(On their own with no protecting garrison or legion)
Formed a great geographic domain called New Netherlands.
Those settlements were the beginnings of cities and hinterlands.
His voyage was important for each future generation
And his discovery was part of the great foundation
For building the colonies which formed one nation.

Dutch Settlements in the 1600s

Hudson's explorations up the North River brought him to a great valley,
Where a friendly riverside-dwelling tribe, the Mahicans, hunted and traded beaver.
He traded with the locals and received beaver pelts which, after a careful tally,
He loaded on the ship in heavy bundles, lifted by a sailor, a very strong heaver,
And then hoisted up on to the deck
And sent to the hold after an inspection check.
On his return voyage, he brought back the wares to Holland,
Examples of what was available in the new land.
Beaver furs handled water well, and when they dried they were as good as new,
And the Dutch were happy with the wares that came into their view.
All over Europe there was great demand clothing made of beaver:
The fur was highly prized for coats and hats
And unlike with wool, there was no need for a weaver.
The furry winter clothes, a great surprise to people and even to curious dogs and cats.

This piqued the interest of the business-minded Dutch,
A venturesome people who would try things others would not touch.
Very interested in the manufacture and trading of goods,
They were not averse to a product that came from the streams and the woods,
But it was from a world with which they had little connection,
Where to survive from natives you needed protection,
So it seemed like a shaky enterprise
Very likely to meet an early demise.
However, the was a need for warm outerwear in central and northern climes,
And elegant furs were appealing in those times.

About four years later, the Dutch established a trading post in Albany
They were high up in the hills—it must have felt like a balcony,
And all around the area stood trees of fir
And strong river breezes their branches would stir.
In tree-covered mountains in the darkness of night
The only illumination was the moon shining bright,
And to the traders the place must have seemed outlandish,
And in response to threats their own weapons they would brandish.

The Dutch would trade European-made goods and wampum for fur.
In trading, values were agreed on and no balance would incur.
The former they paid few and the latter they received many—
There was something about the interests of each party that was uncanny.
There were utilitarian benefits and other advantages the business conferred:
It helped the Indians with tribal support and maintenance cares.
The Mahicans were happy to market their hunting wares
And to receive the goods from Europe they preferred,
As with them they had a higher standard of living,
And the Indians would share the goods with each other in a custom of giving.
Hitherto, they'd had to visit remote locations in the beaver trade,
Looking for opportunities as business was only ho-hum
Traveling to Manhattan and Long Island, they traded with local Indians for wampum.
Harvested mainly along the barrier islands, wampum was like jewelry: in those days
The Indians used it to dress up for festivities and tribal functions on holidays.
You could say it was a fair trade: river valleys had beaver and seashores had shells,
So there was an economic benefit in the trade, as history clearly tells.

In 1621, the Dutch West India Company was established with top priority.
For the new settlements, the new business provided the authority.
The first Dutch settlers came in May 1624,
Establishing trading posts along the shore
Where goods were easy to pick up and deliver:
Fort Nassau and others sprang up near ocean or river.
Off the Delaware River was the island of Verhulsten,
A place that was encountered on the voyage of Hudson;
In Connecticut, Kievits Hoek (now called Old Saybrook);
All told, thirty Dutch families came according to history books,
And they originally landed on the island of Noten,
Today called Governor's Island, off the tip of Manhattan,
Not very far from the barren island of Staten.

When the Dutch settled in the area, their livelihood was the beaver trade,
A business in which many a fortune was made.
They needed to transport the product down the Hudson in a southerly direction.
On that route they could be a target of marauding Indians so they needed protection.
Some of the attacking Indians were Iroquois, the archenemy of the Mahican,

And each side had strong resolve that the other could not weaken.
Iroquois bands crossed the foothills
Of a mountain range called the Catskills,
A natural barrier between the archenemies in ancient rivalry,
Where frictions between the two often erupted violently.
Armed with tomahawks, knives, and bows and arrows,
The Iroquois crossed in certain sections where the river narrows
They could easily reach the river from their territory in the west
And put the shaky relations between the two to the test.
In Lower Manhattan the settlers built a fort
Very close to the great North River's mouth
And not far from Staten Island (a largely uninhabited place to the south),
And named it Fort Amsterdam after the city in the Netherlands
And indeed, a fort was needed because of roving Indian bands.
The fort was located at the tip of Manhattan facing the estuary, next to Upper Bay.
At the entrance to the North River it was essential to build a port.
The subsequent settlement was built in lower Manhattan around and beyond the fort,
And a wall was constructed on its northern border, the Wall Street of today.

The settlement of New Amsterdam thrived on the beaver trade,
The local economy burgeoned with trade with Europe
Even though occasional conflicts with Indians would flare up
And it was that business from which many local workers were paid

After the Dutch settlers came to the New World,
(A foray into the unknown that was very bold,
Gaining for their country an important foothold)
And built Fort Amsterdam in 1625,
A small beginning for a place that would thrive.
Neighboring areas, including Brooklyn, the Dutch would settle,
And moving into uncharted territories was a test of their mettle.
The earliest settlement in Brooklyn, however, was by English people:
In 1645, Gravesende was established as a land of patroons
Under the auspices of Lady Deborah Moody, an Anabaptist
Who had to flee England because of the religion she practiced.
She and her followers built a church with its own steeple.
The English by history were an insular people,

Favoring the seaside where the weather wasn't so harsh;
The land was mostly flat but descended into a marsh,
And over that settlement shined many moons
In the home of snow geese and common loons.

The area was divided into forty-one parcels of land;
An empty place consisting mostly of marshes and sand.
Near the sea, in winter you were less cold and in summer you would not swelter—
It was on oasis of English order in the Dutch world of helter-skelter.
And there was an English attitude without hems and haws,
And there were strict zoning laws.

Her settlement was in the southeastern area by Jamaica Bay.
Opposite Gravesend was a narrow island,
A sandbar called Coney Island just beyond the marshland,
Which was Gravesend Common in that day.

Neighboring Brooklyn Dutch settlements were also founded
In a territory whose borders were generally rounded,
Including Bushwick, Brooklyn, New Utrecht, Flatbush, and Flatlands
In the lands of the roaming Indian bands.
These areas had hosted Dutch settlers since the early days
And the customs established were their own ways.
They were officially established as settlement areas in the 1640s, the era.
Homesteads had comforts: like open-hearth fireplaces, bringing the warmth nearer.

It is interesting to compare the Dutch and British colonial models.
The Dutch colonial ventures were run by a business company from Holland:
Dutch settlers to their homeland were like a child that the mother coddles.
They had limited governmental resources with no military protection
And their borders were thus much more subject to correction.
There were frequent encroachments and attacks by one or another Indian band
So the leader was somewhat like a warlord,
Leading the settlers in battles against the Indian horde.
The English colonial building was fundamentally different in its foundation:
A more complete investment in the future of our yet-unborn nation.
Treating the colonial settlements as an extension of England,

And against external threats always taking a stand,
They built a proper infrastructure, providing services in full complement,
Including militias and an administration for governance to implement.
History shows that the method of the English was sound and longer-lasting;
You could say that their customs were time-honored and from the old school,
And with their method a better outcome you would be forecasting,
Assuring the preeminence of the English legacy long after the end of colonial rule.
It is ironic that the English with militias settled among the peaceful Algonquians
Who generally maintained cordial relations with the Europeans
While the Dutch were near the bellicose Iroquois, with less defense,
Where the competition was decidedly more intense.
The Dutch model was flimsy and easy to fracture,
Placing the settlers on a track less sure.
As it turned out, the Dutch could handle attacks by hostile native bands:
In those situations they would muster a defense with their own hands.
But settlers could not withstand the threat of any major colonial power,
And as history unfolded this became apparent one day in less than an hour.

The English Succession

Since the Late Middle Ages, European countries had a history of seafaring traditions.
Much commerce was conducted over the seas and less over land,
Which was more hazardous and subject to unfavorable conditions.
In those days, a country's trading success and military powers went hand in hand,
And any review of European history makes that principle easy to understand.
Countries that emphasized mercantilism and trade also focused on exploration,
And indeed the discovery of the New World was widely viewed as a great occasion.

The seventeenth century brought change in Europe's geopolitical world.
For two hundred years, the naval powers had been Italy, Portugal, and Spain,
And on the masts of their ships their flags unfurled.
But toward the end of the 1500s their power was clearly on the wane:
In battles at the time, the English superiority was plain.

In the seventeenth century, there was a change in how the pendulum swayed,
And the English were in a good position to capture an advantage in the shipping trade.
England and the Netherlands emerged as the preeminent merchants:
Each excelled in building ships and each for business enterprises had penchants,
Especially the Dutch, whose innovations
Changed the world of shipbuilding in many nations.
Over time, the ships were becoming stronger and more seaworthy,
And a better ship permitted a longer journey.

Those sailing vessels looked like seafaring towers
Which engaged the water whether the sky was clear or bursting with showers.
In their day, they conveyed an impression of awesome power to say the least,
And they developed trade to new areas including the Far East.
So England and the Netherlands emerged as the seafaring winners
In a competition that had many hopefuls and many beginners,
And the sea trade was developing alongside military naval powers
And each nation had formidable business prowess,
But there were frictions between them,
And it is important to understand from where these did stem.
England had an Anglican religious denomination

While Holland had a Calvinistic orientation,
But that was only a minor source of friction between the nations.
The major issue was competition in the world of mercantilism;
Their main purpose on the seas was trade, so the conflict was seen in that prism.
There were multiple business frictions in colonial trade as well,
Particularly in the Far East where the Dutch dominated,
A circumstance that on British ambitions clearly grated.

In the second half of the 1600s, there was more than one Anglo-Dutch war;
It was a time when two colonial powers were entangled in rancor.
There were multiple areas of conflict,
And free passage on the seas one or another would interdict,
Sometimes close and sometimes remote from each country's shore.
It was difficult to say from one day to the next what would be in store;
It was much like a tug of war, with each country fighting with great determination,
The edge shifting back and forth from one to the other nation.

In 1664, there was an event that would create an upheaval,
The type of maneuver characteristic in times Medieval.
The English monarch, Charles II, ceded territories to the Duke of York, his brother,
A large tract of land that included all of New Netherlands,
So legally that meant that the Dutch lost their rights to New World lands,
For the Dutch colony that momentous event presaged change like none other;
It was the prelude to the Second Anglo-Dutch War and colonial cloture,
With expectation for change in colonial administration in the not-too-distant future.

In New Amsterdam on the morning of August twenty-seventh 1664,
No one could imagine that there was an imminent threat of war.
At that time the population was not more than 2,500 in number,
And the people had just arisen from their nocturnal slumber.
The night watch reported nothing amiss in the night hours,
But brewing in the darkness was a major confrontation between powers,
And the people of New Amsterdam rose to a frightening image in the morning light,
For out on the river was an ominous sight:
Four English warships were anchored in the Hudson River,
Alarming the citizenry; and some with fright would shiver.
Poised to attack the settlement, which was mostly defenseless,

The settlers' military weakness accentuated the gravity of their plight.
The settlement was very vulnerable in morning's first daylight,
And there was general agreement that armed resistance would be senseless.

The director-general of New Amsterdam, Peter Stuyvesant,
Was presented with an ultimatum:
"Surrender or come under attack."
The threat was to be taken as verbatim,
And was a danger to which the Dutch could not turn their back.
There was little else he could do but yield to the English nation;
It was not as if there was a negotiating position, given the situation.
Within less than a month, he'd signed the Articles of Capitulation,
A momentous happening in the New World,
And in the fort and beyond the British flag was unfurled,
And New Amsterdam was renamed New York.

So, without a single cannon shot ringing out in the air
From either ship or land battery,
And in the absence of any credible alternative strategy,
And with not much hand-wringing or despair,
There was a change in the administration that was done with care.
A commander of the frigates, only the night before appearing on the scene,
Served as administrator in the interim,
But the English soon sent a coterie of officials to replace him.
People finding change difficult to understand sought any news they could glean,
And after all that had transpired and the change that had come about,
There lingered much perplexity and doubt:
For although there had been a change in the place's name,
The people and their businesses were much the same.
While it is true that the English did abruptly grab power,
That new reality settled in people's minds within an hour.
However, change developed very slowly as the town was Dutch,
And for a considerable period, English settlers avoided it as such
But as time moved on, the English came to New York
And, at dinner, settlers from different lands properly used knife and fork
As they sat in the dining room around the table near the hutch.
There was no shortage of subjects about which to talk

And the Dutch came to live with the English
And the English came to live with the Dutch,
And as for friction between the two, there was really not much.
Soon, a new amalgam was forged whose elements were difficult to distinguish,
A happening rarely seen in history,
But in the New World, there was scarcely any commotion over such.
Each party had much to gain and little to relinquish,
And the benefits of the arrangement were certainly no mystery.

From Isolated Sandbar to Entertainment Island

On the day the Dutch settlement had just begun
And they'd sought their place under the north Atlantic sun,
Coney Island was a barren shifting sandspit
With very little to draw your attention to it.
In winter it had no coat of trees to don,
And the native Indians had mostly gone.
At the time, you could call the place an outcast,
Looking backwards to its distant past
And reverting to its state in pre-human days
With no human influence to change its ways.
During and after the Dutch administration,
The place featured mostly desolation.
People did not live on the island;
There were no homes with fences of white pickets
Which wet weather would splinter,
And it saw only occasional use in winter
When cattle, horses, oxen, and hogs
Grazed there on the dunes and in the thickets,
Starting their days amid the early morning fogs,
As Coney Island was warmer than any mainland island,
Manhattan, Brooklyn, and Long Island,
Since it was lying in the warmer waters of the bay
During the day, no matter what was the time.
But for many, its remoteness outweighed its warmer clime
And that was the principal reason people stayed away.

Coney Island evolved as a single sandbar
From several smaller islands, each from the others not far.
Over time, the sands shifted and the islands coalesced.
Together they gradually became melded;
It was as if together they were welded,
And with one large island the area was blessed.
The geographic character of Coney Island was changing
And its structural alteration was far-ranging,

Partly due to human interventions
Done with the best intentions,
Like filling the flats and carving out waterways
Between the land-based pathways.
Canals connected the creeks for transportation,
Allowing for water-borne navigation
To the place on whose shore the plover plays
In all seasons, on cloudy or sunny days.

In the early days after the independence of our nation
And after that for at least another generation,
The island slumbered deep in reverie,
With hardly any people and no boardwalk or quay.
The island was very quiet just about every day,
But there were some exceptions to the general rule, you could certainly say:
Some people preferred the beach and the sea—
For them that was the place to be—
Amid the seemingly endless sands
And the small creeks and the open bay,
There was no place they would choose to be instead.
The population was limited to only a few intrepid souls and their families
Braving the treeless landscape and the ocean southerlies
Living on the island in a homestead.
The families lived off the land as best they could;
Most did fairly well considering where they stood,
Adopting good spirits and banishing frustration,
But they were isolated from society in that remote location,
Much more isolated than any resident of the mainland for many centuries before,
When the place was reached by canoe and oar.

In that remote setting, only a few children were born and bred,
And about that era and later times the following could be said:
Any child bred on the island was a child of the beach,
A child of the seashore in all seasons,
With great beach insight for many reasons.
With unique experiences and knowledge of the place to teach,
That child would develop a much better understanding than any visitor of the day,

And the background of a native sometimes changes history,
Producing a person who becomes a beach visionary,
And indeed, such a person rose up from childhood on the sand,
Changing the face of the island near the end of the century,
Building creations that were even greater than grand.

Interest in the island increased when access did improve,
And the place started to slide into its proper groove.
That first happened when a bridge was built over Coney Island Creek
Connecting mainland and island, whose summer weather you would seek.
Most people were attracted to the mildness of the summer clime.
The bridge was built in 1829, and some development started at that time,
Bringing to the area a renewed sense of meaning and pride.
Shell Road was built from the western end to the eastern side.

Then came the first hotel, Coney Island House near Sea Gate,
In the shelter of a beach, worthy lodging with grace
With comforts of home and seaside dining without much wait
And if you came from Manhattan after a half-day trip you did not come late.
Carriage roads were built and steamships would sail to the place
Over the course of the next decade,
And memories of the island's isolation began to fade.
In the mid-century, development was increasing its pace;
Ferries brought you to Norton's Point at the western tip,
And the ride was smooth as the seas were tranquil in that land-protected space.
After the Civil War, resorts sprang up at a rapid clip:
Brighton Beach (an adjacent area to the east) was founded
And Manhattan Beach, just to its east, followed that and all was smooth sailing
With upscale resort accommodations prevailing,
Making the island facilities much more well-rounded.
The development of the railway in that era
Brought travelers directly to the island, a great success
Bringing the prospect of development even nearer.
For the island, it was a major factor in opening up access.

Excursion railroads and the Coney Island & Brooklyn Railroad streetcar line
Reached the island in the 1860s, and the ride was just fine,

But that was the beginning of a competition
In which there was little repetition,
And each developer looked for a unique place under the sun
And devised something new, not to be outdone.

As development increased, the area saw the arrival of a new line.
It was built with all the modern railroad features in the year 1889
And was named after Andrew R. Culver, its president.
A welcome development, a joy to the city for any visitor or resident,
You could take the Prospect Park and Coney Island Railroad for thirty-five cents.
With a fare so reasonable, the trip made a lot of sense
To the Surf Avenue Terminal, near the beach, in the center of it all.
When you arrived there, you could hear adventure's call.

To promote the development of the island as an area of beach resorts,
Three vacation areas were built in the same era, and the builders spared no efforts:
Coney Island, Brighton Beach, and Manhattan Beach, each with its own devotees,
Favoring sandy beaches and cool breezes from the sea,
And by the early 1900s, business was booming
And even greater economic development was looming.
The island was teeming with visitors, whatever the merits of the shores and the seas,
You could tell even without a blue-ribbon panel of business conferees;
Shoreline hotels, the Iron Tower, and the amusement parks
From which excitement and joy of summer entertainment sparks.
The beach, the parks, the concessions: all were a great sensation
That made the area the summer capital of the nation.
The Iron Tower was three hundred feet high
And it seemed almost to touch the sky.
It was brought to the island from the 1876 Philadelphia Exposition
Where it was dismantled and then reassembled in good condition.

There were private bathhouses and vaudeville theaters on the island.
For a vacation the place was affordable, not pie-in-the-sky land.
There was a multitude of possibilities on the island's every mile,
And a remarkable change came to the island after such a long while.
At the turn of the twentieth century and into the first and second decade,
Boatloads of immigrant came past the island where shorebirds wade,

Immigrants from eastern and southern Europe came in very large numbers.
That event in history was a great stimulus for the development of Coney Island.
In the summer, if you lived in the city, the beaches were the place to be
For relaxation and merriment on the shore of the sea.
It was a place of involvement and action that you could call not-to-be-shy-land,
And it was considerably cooler than just about anywhere else in those two boroughs,
Due to the strong ocean breezes, even with plenty of sun and hardly any shadows.
People were attracted to the beaches and the amusement parks
Where to songs of sirens of entertainment the listener patiently harks,
And it all started to come together and appear—
Around 1880 was the year.

A Carousel on Coney Island

The era of the amusement parks began in 1876 with a carousel.
That merry-go-round was one that children loved and came to know well;
It was installed on West 6th and Surf at Vandeveer's bath house complex,
And had lovable patient steeds that you could under no circumstances vex.
It was the creation of a Danish woodcarver, Charles Looff,
And had hand-crafted wooden horses that were never aloof.
The musical accompaniment was supplied by a flutist and a drummer,
And the carousel was the busiest place on the island in summer.
It was covered by a sturdy wooden tent top
And the tickets to ride were a nickel a pop.
There was a projecting wooden arm that treasure could bring
From which you could snatch either an iron or a gold ring.

The carousel ride was a model for many other rides to come
Which would bring merriment, adventure, and then some.
Very different from the fast-moving rides with motion-borne wrath,
It slowly moved with musical accompaniment in a circular path.
The carousel was a comfort and a joy to young ones—
Again and again it would go around in several runs.
The musical piece would come to an end
And the carousel slowly stopped at a particular bend.

So you could bring the youngsters for a fun-filled interlude;
For a wooden horse is always in an agreeable mood.
The adventure of a ride was fun for girls and boys,
Providing a needed respite from motionless toys
And the horse never behaved like the proverbial ornery cuss
And, generally smiling, never put up any fuss.
Stationary and often attached to the tented roof's truss
And rarely needing coaxing to move,
The horses could excite or sooth.

The carousel had an impressive polished look, with steeds standing with great poise
As if removed from hills, meadows, and moors.

Coney Island

Planted in the midst of Coney Island's grand outdoors
With bay breezes, sun, and plenty of noise.
Adding to the festivity, the carousel was encircled by parents shouting cheers,
And the music would overcome the sound of its motor and gears,
Which under the platform were found,
And turned the circular base round and round.
With frequent use, there was the expected creaking sound
And an occasional screech and an unavoidable rattle
And the music hushed the din of young children's prattle.

There were people, mostly kids, on the ride,
And smiling faces and gleeful shouts came from every side,
While a ring of bystanders stood around it.
You could get on the ride at any bordering location
And finding your favorite steed
Was a cause for great elation.
On its wooden saddle you would hope to sit,
But you had to put on some speed
As there was a prize for the speedy winner,
And the tranquil ride you could easily endure after dinner
And you would hardly ever want to quit.

The carousel was a modest beginning
That could be considered only the first inning,
But later came many fun-filled and exciting rides
Arriving with a big splash with the island's tides.

But later for an eleven-year-old, a carousel was a ride of old fame;
There was something new that could easily rival all the bullfights in Spain.
It offered more adventure than any spectator game
And the place was widely accessible by subway train.
Indeed, a ride on the Cyclone made a bicycle seem tame—
If you missed that spectacular ride it would be a shame.

There were three major amusement parks in Coney Island
Which seemed constantly in motion like dancing muses,
Whose rides were inviting to even the most dedicated recluses:

Alan Balsam

Luna Park, Dreamland, and Steeplechase Park
Were open seven days a week in daylight and dark
And in their heyday, those and many an independent amusement ride
Attracted several million visitors a year and were a national pride.

George Cornelius Tilyou

Young master George Tilyou
Was born in the year 1862
To Eileen and Peter Tilyou.
Peter had worked in Manhattan as a city recorder
And he was looking for a business opportunity
Not in a remote location but rather within the local community.
One came up just off of Brooklyn's southern border
That was an opportunity Peter felt he could not ignore.
It involved leasing land inexpensively on the seashore.
Sensing a chance to improve the living standards of their family,
Peter and Eileen moved to Coney Island when George was only three.

In 1865, the year they moved, there was a major development in transportation:
The steam-powered railroad had arrived in Coney Island.
The Brooklyn, Bath, and Coney Island Railroad, a moving sensation,
Ran to the West End Terminal, bringing you to the gateway to the sea.
For businesspeople it offered the prospect of pie-in-the-sky-land.
They leased a lot with three hundred feet of ocean front
And a view beyond the bay as far as you could see.
The yearly lease cost thirty-five dollars, a sum that created business opportunity.
On that lot they built Surf House, a solid structure to bear any storm's brunt.
It was a convenient place as the railroad station was within reach
And it attracted many enthusiasts of the beach
Including workers with blue and white collars.
A tavern that was well-known for service with grace
In the model of a mom-and-pop business place:
For the ambience, location, and food, people willingly paid their dollars
And they also rented bathing suits and bath house space.
A boon to the visitor escaping humdrum work into recreation's relaxing pace.

Peter Tilyou built his inn and tavern on the beach near the station.
He reasoned that the business would prosper there
For the people of Brooklyn and Manhattan
Had access to rapid transit to that place.

He could not attract people from the districts of silk and satin
But as a large number of working people would come, he did not care,
And he soon learned that the upper crust he should not chase.
Formerly an isolated place in the nation,
Coney Island was becoming a busy destination,
Such was the prospect that presented itself to Tilyou.
There was no need send out invitations to come asking: *Will you?*
You could see why he wanted that venture under his wing;
It had the ingredients for great success,
And all of its elements signaled progress,
Which in short order became the very same thing.

George had an entrepreneurial spirit as well—
From even a short encounter with the child you could tell.
At age fourteen he sold small boxes of authentic beach sand,
Which he cranked out deftly with only one hand,
And small bottles of genuine Atlantic salt water to tourists—
The terms "authentic" and "genuine" were appealing to purists.
In those days the island was mostly sand,
Piled high with seashells unlike the mainland,
And the waters of the bay had mixed with the ocean and were salty.
Young George was very familiar with the wilderness of the beach
And the emptiness of the island had much to teach
And he had ideas to correct anything man-made that was faulty.
George grew up around the family's enterprises
And learned that in business there are always surprises
That come sometimes as often as the sun rises
On the beach, in a tavern, or at the bath houses.
And to the geniuses of mercantile enterprises
Any void in the market the acumen always rouses.

As a teenager he saved up to buy a horse,
A dream of any young lad of the day, appealing of course,
And so beloved to him was the trusty steed
That it gave him the inspiration to fulfill a business need.
He acquired another and built a beach stagecoach from driftwood,
Adding as many practical features as he could,

And in the process he rapidly learned how to fashion a dovetail joint.
He started a shuttle service bringing visitors from Norton's Point,
Some seeking to escape from the shadows of the city's tenement cavern
To Culver Plaza near the family tavern.
He bought another coach and ran both from one to the other destination
And many people looked for the lad when they arrived at the station.

At the age of seventeen, he ventured into real estate
With his brother Edward as his partner in business.
Both he and his brother were very ambitious
And for their first opportunity they did not long have to wait.
It was the mainland in Brooklyn in Gravesend of today
In a neighborhood in the vicinity of Ocean Parkway.
The business involved the sale of property leases
As since the time of the patroonship of old
No land could be sold or cut up into pieces
But it could be leased and the leases could be sold.

George also became interested in Vaudeville
A live form of entertainment that was a great thrill
And a very popular entertainment trend,
So he and his father conceived of a venture that would fill the till
And together they built Coney Island's first theater.
It was a great achievement, a tribute to the business's creator,
Not far from the island's southern end.
Tilyou's Surf Theater rose on a street they carved out.
Between Surf Avenue and the beach, equidistant about,
On a street they called Bowery Street,
And alongside the theater there were bars and restaurants
Where locals residents and visiting tourists would come to meet,
And the activity day and night attracted bon vivants.

Not long afterwards, when it became legal to buy and sell real estate in Gravesend,
George went back into that business and was a great success.
For most upscale people, the location was a great address,
And he was a good salesman and took advantage of the new trend.
However, he and his father were perennially fighting City Hall,

As when problems arose, that was not the place to call—
It was in the hands of a political machine
That took advantage of the business scene,
Giving the impression that it was always on the take
With one hand in the business till,
Meddling in business for its own sake,
Stirring up trouble with the rowdy, the ruffian, and the rake,
So that in local business there was no such thing as a fair shake,
An arrangement with which the citizenry had their fill.
They and many others were members of a reformist group
That succeeded in changing things in one fell swoop.

George had a penchant for showmanship,
A tendency that led him into a new business enterprise.
Most people greeted the venture with considerable surprise,
Wondering whether it would ever survive.
But to the contrary, it was destined to thrive under his stewardship,
One that highlighted his great imagination and enterprise.
At the time people thought it was a work only a magician could contrive.
It was considered too unusual to win any prize
As it was unfamiliar to people and in its infancy at the time,
Requiring skills and creativity that were soon to be in their prime.
The venture was in the amusement park business
And it turned out to be a new road to riches.

It all started with imaginative business ambitions and obsessions
To secure profitable locations with concessions,
A potpourri of freelance attractions and rides
That later would be part of the amusement park as well as at its sides.

The first ride was modelled after George Ferris's great wheel,
A colossal figure made entirely of steel.
People would ride in cabins dangling in the air,
And the ride was an attraction without compare.
As a legacy of that magnificent wheel,
Similar models were constructed for many a country fair.
The wheel was 125 feet in diameter and twelve cabins it bore,

And the prospective passenger had no idea what was next in store.
Each cabin could give eighteen passengers nestled inside
An unparalleled adventure and a joyous circular ride
From the land to the heights and back again,
A trip with many exciting sights repeating like a refrain.
Riders were treated to views of the bay and the ocean beyond
And the expanse of Brooklyn, the sight of which you'd be very fond,
The cabins would rotate and slide
And you felt all that motion while inside—
It all happened with great quickness
And it was not for people prone to motion sickness
As that malady could easily develop in that setting
And against that possibility, it was not worth betting.

Soon, Tilyou the younger had the idea of bringing many attractions
Together in one place and charging a single admission fee.
It was a good thought that would allow for expansions and contractions
And it would be worthwhile to invest to build a park near the sea.
It seemed like a business that was sure to thrive;
The model was established in 1895
By Captain Paul Boyton who founded the nearby Sea Lion Park,
Which was so popular it was open from early morning till dark,
A place you could put common folk and the wealthier in;
It was such a great attraction that it drew much attention.
It had a water toboggan ride called Shoot the Chutes
And on that ride your feet would stay dry even without long boots.

The plan from a business standpoint was a great advance,
As it provided a savings for customers and so had the best chance.
You could try just about any ride for only twenty-five cents,
An arrangement most people thought made a lot of sense.
So, between Surf Avenue and Bowery Street,
On fifteen acres to the east and the west, set out in a pattern quite neat,
Rose an adventure land called Steeplechase Park.
The sign displayed the broadly grinning face of a jester,
A spectacular sight that would have amazed any visitor's ancestor.
Illuminated by the sun in the day and lights in the dark,

It proudly proclaimed in very large letters, *Geo. C. Tilyou*,
The name of its proprietor and founder.
It was in the pattern of promotional hype and ballyhoo
So typical of those days,
And successful with the public in many ways.
Compared with others, George's method was sounder:
He created adventure beyond your wildest dreams in a fantastic milieu,
And that sign provided an affirmation
Of the genius of the person responsible for that magnificent creation.
It was, without question, a one-of-a-kind place in the whole nation.

The Wonders of Steeplechase Park

In 1897, George C. Tilyou opened the gates of the park,
And they remained open from early in the day to well after dark.
The centerpiece attraction was a ride on wooden horses,
Gliding along rails on spectacular man-made courses.
Those venerable steeds rode with aplomb and grace
Along the mechanical Steeplechase.

Out of the starting gate riders on horses would roll
On the steel tracks that undulated and propelled them forward.
Heading eastward, westward, southward, or northward,
For them it was easy to fly over yonder knoll
In races over hill and dale.
There was no worry about falling into a hole—
Those galloping steeds with colors dark or pale
With outstretched heads and motionless tails
Coasted along side by side on adjacent rails.
Those mechanical racehorses were great sliders,
A great joy and comfort to their adventurous riders,
Moving with great speed and without any hitch,
And the workings of the apparatus rarely saw any glitch.

Unlike hunting foxes in the country on a sunny day
With loyal hounds that could lead the way,
Running over the countryside without any pretenses,
Able steeds that could easily jump high over fences
To the sound of the bugle peal.
The perils of those races were very real
As the hilly terrain often had an irregular pitch
And one false move could land you in a countryside ditch.

The wooden horses generally had two riders
But sometimes you would see only one
And, depending on the rail location, there were insiders and outsiders.
Either way, all agreed that the ride was a lot of fun.

Other features of the park in the early days
Included adventure-filled rides that kept you in constant motion,
Showing that originality and ingenuity generally pays,
Even without hyperbole and a lot of promotion.
Popular beach staples including a large swimming pool
Were good for kids who needed a break from the routines of school,
And joy pervaded that setting as a general rule,
Where among the happy swimmers there was little commotion.
Compared with the roaring ocean the pool water was gentle,
And it was conveniently located near the bath house for rental.

The park had a small circus exhibition for family fun
With wild animals including tigers, not to be outdone—
Tigers would stand on their rear legs and growl
And their trainer would shout loudly and banish their scowl
And there was a very large ballroom for dancing
And the popular music of the day was slow and entrancing.

Some of the attractions devised by Mr. Tilyou
Presented surprises for which there was no clue,
Reflecting a certain uniqueness and boldness in his approach.
The main idea was to create fun in a social setting
And on a particular outcome it was not worth betting.
Despite embarrassments, his motives were beyond reproach.

His method had some rough edges you could call clownsmanship
But many visitors related to that spirit with a feeling of kinship.
His rides required a person's active participation
And each one was an innovative creation
But you had to find your own way as there was no coach
And when you had no experience you had to quickly develop an approach.
You had to be ready to teeter and totter and even fall
And all that had to be done in a public setting,
And against the possibility of falling it was not worth betting.
Anyway, in that challenge there was no winner's cup—
The important thing was to pick yourself up,
Straighten out the ruffles, and then stand tall.

The first park lasted only about a decade.
Visitors loved that place, including the adventurous and the staid,
And year after year its successes did not fade.
During that time it was a great sensation—
But it fell victim to an island-wide conflagration.
The spirited owner was not discouraged by the tragedy;
He vowed to rebuild a bigger and better park, restoring all its earlier majesty,
So with pen and paper, a prototype he drew
Of an amusement park that would be filled with fun
And rising out of the ruins of Steeplechase I
Came Steeplechase II,
Another spectacular achievement for George Tilyou,
Assuring his great legacy on the island under the sun.
In that park the original rides were rebuilt
And new horses ran on track rails without any tilt
And a new generation came to love the park so well
Some, if they had a choice, would choose to live at a nearby hotel.
The descriptions of the rides presented here
Are designed to be concise and clear
An account that is correct and true
With respect to Steeplechase II.

In the Roaring Twenties prosperity was spreading all over,
Including in Coney Island, the domain of the seagull and plover.
The beach was a destination for city folks
Wishing to put on happy faces
In an amusement park of all places
And to escape the city summer heat.
It was certainly a fun place for people to meet;
You could meet Wilder and William among other folks.
The amusement parks in Coney Island were also a major attraction
For children and adults as places of adventure, fun, and jokes—
For people seeking entertainment they brought great satisfaction.

On a Saturday night, the parks were heavily attended
Under a canopy of stars and the moon shining in the sky.
The parks were places where the vendors of entertainment their trade did ply

And people to frivolity and carefree activities surrendered
In the city, the borough, and the shire.
In those days men dressed in formal attire
Which could be bought or was always available for hire.
A dress suit, a formal long-sleeved shirt, and a tie,
And in summer that often included a white straw hat.
There was much style and elegance in all that.
Ladies wore their hair short or in long tresses
And it was customary to wear ankle-length dresses,
And that is the way they arrived at Tilyou's place,
To enjoy his rides, including Steeplechase.
Whether in the day or the night,
Formal dress was considered right.
After all, it was the aftermath of Victorian times,
Even in the domain of nickels and dimes.

On a Saturday night, to get into the park
You entered through Bowery Street, which was well-lit in the dark.
First you had to get through the Barrel of Love,
Which was a rotating barrel-shaped passageway,
And with several people there could be a push and a shove.
The challenge of getting through that rotating cylinder is hard to gainsay
And there was always some degree of hesitation and fear
As it could certainly sweep you off your feet,
Instantly bringing on a feeling of defeat,
And if you fell it was not clear where you'd be landing
And even with an escort by your side or very near
When all was said and done
There was no guarantee that you would remain standing
As two could fall as easily as one.
Many people preferred to move through that walkway alone
But there was no guarantee that they would not wind up prone.

I would have called the ride Barrel of Fun,
For names make a difference under the sun.
To me that would be a more apt appellation,
For that shining star in G.C.'s constellation

That always shined bright.
But using that name would present a limitation
As to the Pavilion of Fun that passageway led you
And name redundancy was not allowed in the domain of Tilyou.
But by any name it was a great sensation
That prompted almost universal approbation
And when you looked at the faces of the visitors each night
Preparing to take their first step into that twirling tube
(Though wishing that instead it was a slow-moving cube)
You could discern that they showed little hesitation
And there was no yielding to transient fright
That could only worsen your plight.
As entering the park held such a strong allure
(Even though a rotating tube could cause disturbance of station,
A condition for which there was no need for a cure),
There was much great elation
And to get through the barrel not much trepidation.

Once in the interior of the park,
Decisions could be made on a lark
As a matter of design not chance.
You could go to the ballroom to dance
Or head straight for the ever-popular Human Roulette Wheel,
A ride testing your skills you could love head over heel.
Initially, the ride was called the Squeezer,
Fun-filled, it was a true crowd pleaser
In which the individual was separated from the group,
Lost from the comfort and calm of the troop,
Like grazing sheep from the herd as clouds burst over hills
In the light of the moon where the nightingale trills.

A joy of a ride that stirred up great commotion
One that relied on the gradual increase in motion
Of a central spinning platform wheel,
Where many people seated themselves, knees to their chests,
Jockeying for a position they could hold on to best,
Trying to resist the effects of the upcoming spin,

Which would make the central spinning platform difficult to stay in,
And indeed, it was difficult to keep an even keel—
It was like trying to hold on to a moving wheel.
There was a tendency to be cast off by centrifugal forces,
As if one was pulled by a team of strong horses.
It was hard to prevent ejection by the rapid spin
So, not surprisingly, one by one riders fell off to the side,
But occasionally one or two riders remained in their places
The joy of their triumph could be seen in their faces.
Others losing their hold were cast aside,
Fortunately with no real blow to their pride,
A fact that none of the castoffs would try to hide.
Only slightly ruffled, they'd get up and move aside.

Others, after tumbling and rolling through the Barrel of Love
Emerged with the placid demeanor of a dove
And headed straight for a ride that moved in a whirl—
It was one to love whether you were a boy or a girl.
It was officially called the Swings, but also the Flyer,
And you would glide through the air and gradually move higher.
A ride on those swings (one person per swing)
was akin to actually flying, an experience that was no ordinary thing.
Those swings would rotate in a very wide arc
And from there you could easily see outside of the park,
And a slower the visual scan, gave a view that was more thorough
All the way over Brooklyn, the borough
And over the beach into the vastness of Lower Bay.
So hold on to those suspension chains
And gaze at the diversity of the terrain
As through the air the swings smoothly glide
Making this a most adventurous and enjoyable ride.

Another spectacular spinning ride
Was called the Human Pool Table.
Its interested riders were willing and able
To slide on to rotating circular platforms.
One after another, they were delivered in swarms

Dispatched via the Dew Drop slide,
A tower-like contraption at the front side
That rapidly sent you on to twenty-four spinning discs
That all spun in different directions.
The object was to slide across those moving discs,
Moving to the opposite end past various sections.
Most people emerged from the chute on their backs
And then tried to choose sensible tracks,
But it was hard to navigate those spinners
And excitement and fun were the only clear winners.
Many a well-dressed gentleman was split from his hat
(A tumble on the discs would guarantee that)
And women's long dresses would begin to unfurl,
A discomfort to be endured for the sake of greater purpose, the ride
A thing of joy and excitement, not modesty and pride,
But all would agree that pants would have been easier for any lady or girl.
Rising to one's feet on spinning round platforms was no easy trick,
Even if your balance was good and your reflexes were quick.

At the Turn of the Century

The beginning of the twentieth century
Witnessed great change in New York City:
Immigrants from Eastern Europe and Italy
Arrived and the local population did swell,
And stories of their experiences they would tell.
The city was at the center of that epic relocation
And the influence of that migration
Was subsequently felt across the nation.

Starting two decades before the arrival of the new century,
People came to the United States to fulfill their dreams
In a land where the radiant light of bounty gleams.
To build a new life in a country that offered great opportunity,
Some came alone but others with families
From diverse starting points along the shores of European seas.
They often came by cargo ship,
Making it a very difficult trip—
Ships were crowded and there were few amenities.
Many people sailed in steerage class
And for most there was little choice, alas,
As these ships charged the least expensive fare
But even basic comforts were rare.

When walking on the deck from stern to bow
You'd find an overfilled space,
There was little room to share in that traveling class
So the walk was at a very slow pace.
Any faster would be sure to cause a row
As there was very little room to pass.

On any long voyage you'd meet the furies of the Atlantic Ocean.
The majority of the passengers had never been aboard a sailing vessel,
And many became ill from the ship's incessant rocking motion
During that journey on the perilous and stormy sea,

So there was a need for an apothecary with mortar and pestle
To produce some medicine to alleviate the sea-borne malady.

Ships would arrive in the early morning light
Emerging from the sea in the darkness of night.
The vessels made their way along the Long Island coast;
The new shores were like a gift to a guest from a host.

At the very beginning of the new day,
As you passed the coastal islands and Jamaica Bay,
On the mainland you'd make out an isolated steeple.
One of the first landmarks seen by new people
Was a large structure looming on the beach,
So large that you might stretch out your arm and think it in reach.
Standing on the island was Elephantine Colossus,
A hotel that stood near the shore between 1885 and 1896,
Resembling an elephant but with squared body contours and proboscis.
But after a decade it was gone as history said nix.
Though it was a sensation in its time, it did not have staying power.
For exotic similes the promoters of the day had a penchant,
And the hotel turned out to be the proverbial white elephant.
In its place in 1907, rising high in the air, came Dreamland Tower.
Each in its day was an impressive and imposing sight,
And arriving on the heels of the invention of the electric light,
Their silhouettes glowed in the darkness of the night.

Uprooting from centuries of life in their European homelands,
Coming to the New World in search of freedom and opportunity,
Attracted by tales of great successes in the community,
Immigrants from Europe filled the neighborhoods of New York City,
But there was often fanciful exaggeration in what they told,
Like how the streets of America were paved with gold.
But hyperbole aside, the message behind those stories certainly took hold—
However, many newcomers faced a very different reality
That cast many of those tales into the realm of wishful banality.
They had to contend with several adverse factors before realizing their goal
Depending along which path the wheel of fate would roll.

First, they had to learn the culture and the language of the land;
Many underestimated that impediment as its complexity they did not understand.
For workers seeking employment there was often only variable demand.
The effects of the Industrial Revolution were at an early point in the economy
But there was great hope that things would change and bring financial autonomy.

Initially, many immigrant families had to face adversity
In the setting of overcrowded low-cost housing in New York City.
Sheltered in Lower Manhattan in tenements
Where the crowding had evil portents
In living conditions that were a constant struggle
And snatches of hopes they would yearn to smuggle.

The alleys between the buildings were perennially in the shadows.
The light was blocked by the tall structures of the tenements
And there were dancing images of wind-blown clothes
And the sky was clouded by white clothes and sheets on clotheslines
And bright dreams were overshadowed by darker sentiments.
Visiting nurses frequently encountered malnutrition in those confines
And communicable diseases were rife, especially the consumption.
In that urban setting such were the burdens of the human condition:
On some faces you could see expressions of despair
Rising from a feeling that the plight was beyond repair.
For those individuals it was as if the world did not care;
For others it was time to roll up your sleeves—no use pouting
About lack of comforts in an uncomfortable setting, it was not worth shouting—
To turn the tides of fortune, you had to set your sights elsewhere.
And about that approach, most would agree, there was no doubting.

There was opportunity in small businesses including retail,
But changing circumstances your plans could derail.
And with the coming of modernity and the departure of the horse-drawn shay,
Family-owned shops held sway:
Groceries, convenience stores, haberdasheries, and dressmaker shops,
Where all the wares were stored and displayed on the premises
(The neighborhood businesses of the moms and pops).

In addition, there was plenty of work in services
And in small-scale manufacturing like the garment industry.
A world of progress came with the invention of the sewing machine
Which mostly operated on electricity.
Women did piece work, focusing on very small details,
Helping their families earn a living the reward for their travails.
But factories were overcrowded and lighting was poor in that dreadful scene
And working conditions were sometimes a nightmare,
Reflecting the pains of the industrial revolution, products were made without care
On the second floor of a building in the garment center,
Where the hapless worker was employed and the business-owner was a renter.
Many people started out in that type of employment
Until they could buy a small business of their own
Or, better yet, become involved in a business that was completely unknown.
The foundation of life was work and there was little opportunity for enjoyment.

And at the time there was a lower class and an upper class,
And from the one to the other there was no free pass.
The two were miles apart and there were no levels in between—
The prevailing pattern in the economic and social scene.
Inexpensive comfort items, mass-produced today, were not available at the time,
In the world of the penny, the nickel, and the dime.
In new areas of business there was great opportunity,
And in many areas of the rapidly growing economy
There was a great need for workers in services and industry.

But for achieving success in America there were no guarantees;
In those days there were rags-to-riches stories
But there was a lot in those stories that defies comprehension,
Usually involving hard-working people without much pretension.
A person starts with nothing and achieves something—
Yes, you could literally start with nothing—
No money, no education, and sometimes not even native language skills
And nonetheless manage to fill empty tills.
It usually happened in a new business field where there was no contention
And people happily greeted the book of opportunity's new edition,

Where anything is possible in the world of the unstructured condition.
But the rags-to-riches formula was like a lottery:
It was the subject of dreams but not the way of reality.

Most people were content to accept going wages,
A compromise that was validated in history books' pages.
Though all enjoyed the freedoms that the country offered
And there were many successes where opportunities were proffered,
There was no guarantee of success whatsoever
Despite opportunity in self-employment endeavor.

The immigrants often came with little education
And few professionals were among them,
But that changed with the first-born generation.
Who had abilities from which success would stem.

The large number of immigrant families of marginal means
And the island's entertainment (the price so right)
Meant the place was perfect for families with children and teens.
They were enchanted by the island day and night—
The beach was free and the subway fare five cents,
So a trip to that place made a lot of sense.

These families were key to the success of the island as an entertainment center.
The proprietors of the businesses worked with low profit margin
(An accepted practice with not one dissenter)
And the beach and amusement rides were open—you didn't have to barge in.
In the twenties it was the nickel empire, and in the forties it became the dime empire.
The attractions on the island drew people from all socioeconomic categories
And their adventures on the island were told in many stories.
For the first quarter of the twentieth century, it drew mostly lower-income guests.
People by experience came to know which places they liked the best
And could afford low-cost amusements, and the beach and the boardwalk were free
And the possibilities seemed endless for anyone on that entertainment spree.

The other major attraction was the lower temperature of the seaside places,
Which was not as dependent as the city on the weather's good graces.

Coney Island

Living in the crowded city did not mean lack of isolation;
There was urban loneliness that gripped the city and the nation.
But at the seashore, there was the open air
And a chance to mingle with people and to be free of care,
And the fact that Coney Island was the closest beach and very accessible
Also contributed to the great success of the island fare,
A fact that people agreed was incontestable.
On weekends in the summer the beach and the boardwalk had standing room only
And in those places it was hard to feel lonely
As the activities would grab your attention
And the friendliness of the people was an accepted convention.

The Roaring Twenties

It was a day of hope and optimism,
When great energy and dynamism
Were coupled with culture and creativity.
Off came the shackles of inactivity:
It was a day of invention, industry, and prosperity,
A time like none other in the history of our nation,
When our country cast off many old-fashioned customs and traditions
Which weighed heavily on or actually worsened economic conditions,
Leading to a pattern of recurrent business stagnation.

Abandoning old ways showed profound wisdom without malevolence.
Though rarely acknowledged in that light, it was an act of great benevolence,
Clearing a path for enterprise, replacing a stodgy economic history
With the extremely powerful force of modern industry,
Bestowing the gift of progress on society, starting at the century's conclusion,
And the grand successes were a consequence of the industrial revolution.

It came toward the end of the first quarter of the twentieth century,
A period when tremendous economic potential was realized, and greater opportunity
Than had been achieved in more than the two centuries since the birth of our nation,
Since the pioneers were struggling to gain a foothold, surviving on meager rations.
It was at this time a sleeping colossus emerged from its slumber
To become a world power, reaching a rank that was one in number.
The Roaring Twenties saw an economic boom of spectacular dimensions
Borne on the wings of new inventions
In the aftermath of the industrial revolution
And spectacular new energies brought on evolution:
The automobile replaced the horse-driven carriage
And its smoother ride was difficult to disparage.
An advance that most agreed was very fine,
It happened as fast as Ford could roll its Model T's off the assembly line.
And then soon after came the subway,
A blend of underground and overhead urban railway.
Radio was invented and broadcasted entertainment and information,

To millions of listeners it brought great joy and inspiration
All over the length and breadth of this great nation.

The airplane first took off at Kitty Hawk
It was a great advance about which people would talk,
And later even over the Atlantic Ocean it would take flight.
Architecture displayed unparalleled vision in Art Deco modernism,
A grand statement of architectural talent and individualism.
Skyscrapers of great beauty were built to unparalleled height,
Their exteriors and interiors each a dressed-up sight.
They transformed and beautified the urban landscape
And the buildings changed the city's shape.
Their creators were considered conquering heroes
Deserving of accolades, as their work clearly shows;
Worthy of showers of ticker tape and a splendid parade.
The two major skyscrapers of the era were completed at the end of the decade.
Before them, an early architectural leader, the Flatiron Building was built in 1902,
A spectacular achievement in its day, but it did not receive its due.
Uniquely shaped like a thin triangular wedge
Located on 5th and 23rd Street at the corner's edge,
With twenty-two stories reaching to the sky, in its day it was the tallest,
An architectural dream at the turn of the century,
A prestigious and fitting address for any plenipotentiary.
As the century unfolded, however, among the largest, it soon became the smallest.

But the Roaring Twenties produced its own architectural masterpieces
And over time the height of the skyscrapers increased.
It was as if earlier achievements were merely the past's fading echo
As the new times brought the titans of Art Deco.
But if until the end of the decade you were to wait,
You'd see the Chrysler Building appear in 1928
(And it took about two years to build).
Then the Empire State Building was built,
Which took less than two years and became the tallest building in the city.
It reached dazzling heights, and the air is thin outside its observatory
And you could see far over the mainland and out to sea.

The Art Deco themes in those buildings are an inspiration;
That architectural style became popular throughout the nation.

In the Roaring Twenties, there were still vaudeville productions
At places that were so well known they needed no introductions,
Like at the Palace Theater on Broadway and West 47th Street.
At various locations in the city there were others;
Programs were live and, in 1920, featured the Marx Brothers,
And on stage for an entire year appeared Bessie Clayton,
Whose dancing performances were indeed a great treat
Whether you were from Philadelphia, Cleveland, or Dayton.

At the New Amsterdam Theater played the Ziegfeld Follies
Featuring dancing ladies elegantly dressed in chiffon, lace, and sequins.
Standing with great poise and dancing with gusto, they were glittering dollies
And many vaudevillians took to the stage in the early twenties,
Including Fanny Brice, W.C. Fields, Edie Cantor, and Sophie Tucker,
And people enjoyed the music played by Paul Whiteman and his band.
In tableu vivants appeared the Ziegfeld dancers;
On grand stairway props on the stage they would stand
(In those days grand entrances were all the rage)
And from the heights they would descend to the stage
To perform row dancing, arm in arm, as inspiring as shows at the *Folies Bergere*,
Dancing ladies dressed in spectacular costumes,
With a musical accompaniment of popular vaudeville tunes,
Like the one that glorifies shining harvest moons…
That was vaudeville standard fare
And in the brief skits presented there was not much of a story.
But the acts were favored by audiences of all ages
And well described on the program pages
And tickets to those shows were easy to sell.
At Carnegie Hall in 1925, George Gershwin conducted classical repertory
And jazz musicians and singers performed as well.

But toward the end of the decade, the talkies (motion pictures with talking) arrived,
Replacing silent movies and the vaudeville creation,
A landmark achievement in entertainment, one that was brilliantly contrived,

And the popularity of talking movies swept the nation.
They were a great sensation
And a major new industry was created overnight.
The first talkie to arrive was *The Jazz Singer*.
It was a first and its impact certainly did linger,
And Hollywood proceeded to sound the cash register ringer
With a variety of musical films whose novelty was hard to resist.
It was a popular medium and people made money hand over fist.

The streets of the city were in the process of changing;
Yielding to the needs of the automobile took some rearranging.
The trolley ran along Broadway and traffic became snarled
And the patience of the drivers was tested and their faces became gnarled.
In a few years, the trolley and the tracks had to be completely removed:
It was an anachronism in the era of the automobile, that history proved.
Double-decker buses brought tourists to various sights
And the city was a tourist's delight, dressed up for the holiday,
With alluring streets and places open in the day and night
Or on just about any day of the week, Monday through Sunday.

Theaters and stores were active along Broadway.
During the day and at night
It was a spectacular sight.
Illuminated in the dark, it was called the Great White Way.
At Times Square signs were arranged in a grand display.
Nationwide business enterprises were keen to catch the consumer's eye
And the companies for that advertising space eagerly would vie—
Department stores, coffee purveyors, auto companies and mass producers of the day.

It was the time of times in New York City
The city enjoyed great prosperity.
Consumerism, a child of the twenties, was taking hold.
Horn and Hardart cafeterias were competing with restaurants;
They were called automats, with food that was hot or cold.
You could forget about the kitchen with pans and pots;
Instead, you would put the nickels in the slots
And the windows clicked open and you would lift the glass door

And take out the prepared food
Like halibut with peas and carrots
And apple juice in a bottle, ready to pour.
It was a mother's relief that could feed the family brood—
It was as easy as that—
And so the family in the cafeteria sat.

At the hotels, business was booming
And no one could predict that any change was looming.
The old Waldorf Astoria near Herald Square was in its heyday:
Weekend rooms had to be booked early or you'd have to look elsewhere to stay,
As it was with the Plaza on 5th Avenue and 59th Street.
The Plaza was built in the French Renaissance style, a visual treat.
The Waldorf was soon to be relocated to 5th and rebuilt in Art Deco style.
Each hotel captured the spirit of the period for quite a long while.

The families of the tycoons had grand cottages in Newport,
Where sailing has always been a very popular sport.
On the tranquil, expansive bay the yachts would sail
And in the battle between man and the sea, man would prevail.
Those families moved to New York City
To residential buildings along 5th Avenue,
A great location, bordering on Central Park so pretty,
Where in spring came the first leaf buds and the flowers,
And in summer, relief from oppressive city heat
Was brought by gentle rain showers
And the park's grand hardwood trees which the sun shaded.
The place was not far from alluring retail,
With fancy stores offering the latest fashions for sale
On 5th Avenue below 59th Street,
Where elegance and style were paraded.

The Roaring Twenties witnessed both plenty and scarcity
In the neighborhoods of New York City.
Middle-class people were definitely a rarity,
As rare as earrings with hoops,
And most were part of upper- and lower-income groups.

Between them there was proper civility
But essentially no mobility.
From lower economic status one first had to get to the middle ground,
A process that was a struggle, though the idea was sound.

In the early 1920s, the western world was a study in contrasts;
The ebullience of the times cast aside all gloomy pasts,
But there were excesses and extremes of a self-indulgent class,
Whose self-indulgence was decidedly crass.
It was the world of the sybarite and the smarty
These people wanted life to be a party
Their life was mostly one party followed by the next;
For celebrations, they needed no pretext.
People whose errant ways filled the era's works of fiction.
These hedonists had lost their moral compass
And placed too much emphasis on creating a rumpus,
Feeling that existence had little purpose and too much contradiction.
We should not overemphasize the importance of that vacuous minority
As they were rare exceptions to the principled majority.

Out of the vortex of the Roaring Twenties
Burst a high level of energy that was difficult to suppress,
Bringing notable developments and great progress,
And many lasting achievements the era did witness.
There was a remarkable journey from empties to plenties,
And in art, architecture, and music, there were spectacular creations.
In the world of entertainment, there were many sensations,
And the era was known for its great style and class.
Buildings were constructed that almost touched the sky,
And conventions of size and style they would defy,
And inside them shined marble and brass
And Art Deco motifs with grandeur and intricacy.
The twenties left an important legacy
Of hard-working people with positive mindsets
Willing to try new things rather than fret
And they advanced society for future generations
And even today we enjoy their creations.

New York City in the 1940s and 1950s

It was a time of recovery from two world wars,
Each fought away from our continental shores,
And a great depression came in between
And sweeping changes approached the scene.
You could get a glimpse of new products at the 1939 World's Fair,
Which would permit you to see what the future had to share:
Televisions, washing machines, dryers, and better cars would soon be arriving,
Improving the standard of living, a goal toward which people were striving.

It was also a time for education, which had been delayed by World War II.
It was a time to build infrastructure as well;
The roads of era were advanced, with features that were new,
And came just in time as the population began to swell.
Some roads were elevated and there arose flying junctions,
Where traffic in different directions would cross in the air.
Promoting the flow of traffic and safety were the principal functions;
You would think that in order to do that, cars would have to fly,
An unlikely prospect, but you could easily explain why,
And on the new highways heavy traffic was exceedingly rare.
Day trips by automobile were much shorter to just about anywhere
And the eastern beaches on the Atlantic were even more accessible.
The yearning to spend time at the beach was irrepressible;
There was magic in the combination of sun, sand, and sea.
It was an era that was short on talking and long on doing;
There was much to be done and people rolled up their sleeves to work.
There was a trend to put in a lot of effort and not to shirk.
They began the journey on the long road to recovery,
One that would ultimately lead to great discovery
And there was success in the offing that clearly was brewing.
People did things for themselves, a very healthy approach,
And with little hesitation, a custom beyond reproach.

The times also favored rebuilding and education,
A trend that swept the entire nation.

There was little disagreement that it was the right prescription
And almost every citizen shared that conviction.
It was a recipe for building future success
Which could only happen with government initiatives and largesse.

It was the American way: independence and self-reliance,
A model devised by the pioneers and advanced by generations to follow
After the bonds with Europe were severed in revolutionary defiance
In the land of hills and valleys, rivers and streams, the eagle and the swallow.

Summer at Home and on the Balsam Farm

At home on 94th Street and 101st Avenue, in Ozone Park,
After spring arrived, bringing the robin and the meadowlark,
The sounds of children at play could be heard till dark
On the sidewalks and tree-lined streets and in the park.
The new freedom from winter's reclusiveness was being enjoyed
And people's spirits were certainly buoyed.

Our neighborhood expected a visitation from summer
And the prospect of recreation, a community joy for all to share.
But these arrivals would not be heralded with any fanfare—
No parade or marching band with bugler, fifer, and drummer.

In that season, the city bristled with heat
And escaping its clutch was no easy feat.
In the early days, torrid weather lasted from daybreak till dark.
The sun's rays were intense and the asphalt became warm,
And its heat rose above the city streets like an extended arm
Reaching up from the lowlands all the way to the highlands
With the entire area in its hold, even the wide grassy park
And many discomforted residents would seek refuge in the islands.

From a situation in which refuge is sought at every turn,
There is often much that you can learn.
Frequently things are not as bad as they might seem,
An idea featured in an escape from reality in a summer's winter dream
In which various opposites did at once interact,
And many people the idea in the dream would certainly attract.
During the heat of a summer night the dream did unfold
With a paradoxical theme: a different season's story was told.
One morning, a bedroom chill signaled that frost had taken hold
And the neighborhood outside was enveloped by cold.
Peering out the window, I found the neighborhood covered in snow.
And there were icicles dripping from the window sill
Glaring in the sun and like a statue very still.
Snow was piled high in the backyard.

How the cows fared in the storm was what every Balsam child wanted to know
And on the wall's corkboard hung a seashore scene on a picture postcard
And oddly enough at that time you'd happily think of summer joys at the beaches
And then you'd wake in the sweltering heat
Realizing that a trip to the beach was an easy feat
As one block to the east was Woodhaven Boulevard,
The gateway to the Atlantic shore, which could easily bring you within its reaches.

In summer evenings in Ozone Park, the heat was generally lingering.
Zephyrs from the north swept over Woodhaven hills with muted voice,
Heading in a southerly direction to Jamaica Bay,
Bringing welcome relief, a cause to rejoice,
And the ocean breezes traveled inland over the bay.
For respite from the heat many people would spend the evening outdoors;
One popular subject of discussion was the day's baseball game scores.
It was common to see people seated in front of their houses
With their neighbors enjoying the outdoors and mingling
And children excited about a visit to the circus of Brothers Ringling.

Indoors there was little relief from the heat
And air conditioning was a future developmental treat.
In those days small window units in a house's side
Cooled the rooms, and were neither long nor wide.

And in summer you could surely say
That on any sunny day
Without any shadow of a doubt,
Neighborhood residents wanted to be out
And all roads led to the Atlantic beaches.
Traffic was heavy along Woodhaven Boulevard
And you could easily hear it from any backyard
And frequently hear car brakes' screeches.
There was no question that as you came close to the coast
The temperature dropped—you were the guest and the ocean breezes the host.
It was reminiscent in many ways
Of very different days:
Of the first cool autumn breeze,

A seasonal harbinger of change
Signaling the departure of the songbirds to another geographic range
From the leafy canopies of the neighborhood trees.

The situation was very different on the Balsam Farm:
The family's dairy, with three hundred cows,
Was a family center with great charm
Over which the sun gleamed and spread its beams.
For the family children it was a magical place with many wows,
The birthplace of a thousand and one dreams.

In Ozone Park of today (Lower Woodhaven of the past), near Jamaica Bay,
A lower temperature was an unexpected but welcome guest
And often you'd feel dampness in the morning or late in the day.
Respite would come as the sun made its descent into the west.

The Balsam Farm barns faced the north
Out of which the storms of winter came forth.
They were solidly built structures, barns for all seasons
Modelled after central European examples for many reasons.
These were essential in the north due to the winter's cold
And in the barns' configuration there are many stories to be told.
The cows were kept on the first story and above were bales of hay,
And the back of the barns faced the unseen bay
There were openings in the structures: very large windows and doors
Which admitted the breezes you could feel from the platform floors.

And in a building opposite the barns next to the bottling plant
There was a refrigerated room for milk storage.
Where staying more than a few minutes was difficult to endure;
Even with layers of wool over a flannel shirt it took great courage,
And in summer the room took on a new allure.

But for respite from the city's summer heat
And an evening's entertainment by local folks reckoning
A trip to the bay was a real great treat,
A visit to the carousel on Broad Channel would often be beckoning.

The Carousel on Broad Channel

There is a general rule, easy to understand,
That the shortest distance between two points is a straight line,
And in many fields, including clothing fashion that notion is considered grand,
And so rulers are needed by the tailor crafting a cuff or hem.
However, when it comes to places and the roads that bring you to them,
That rule mostly does not apply, and builders follow a different trend.
There is no telling just how streets and avenues will wend,
As there are too many places one next to another
(Though the situation was worse in the days of your grandmother).
In city neighborhoods and sections,
Streets often head in various patterns, meandering in different directions.

However, there's an exception from Ozone Park to the Rockaway:
Crossbay Boulevard, a very wide thoroughfare,
Goes straight to Broad Channel, an island in Jamaica Bay,
And the straightness of the road brings you there with time to spare.

As a child of five, I knew the island very well,
Mainly because of a superb attraction in that location
Called the Carousel on Broad Channel.
It was a world unto its own,
A world of motion and music, a magical place, a great sensation.
For neighborhood children, it was a place of great renown.

The island was also distinguished by its long and thin shape,
Giving it the character of a cape.
It was like an outstretched arm pointing to Rockaway
Right in the center of Jamaica Bay,
Whose gentle waves coming and going,
Sometimes coalescing in a circular pattern
Like the rings around the planet Saturn.
Exactly where the waves would head, there was no way of knowing.

Alan Balsam

The sunset in the west brought the twilight,
And the sun's last rays of the day
Spread over the tranquil waters of the bay,
Ushering in the velvet night
And the cool breezes of the bay
Seemed to be always coming your way
And sometimes gusts you would meet,
Bringing relief from the summer evening's heat.

When you reached Broad Channel,
After getting off Cross Bay Boulevard,
You'd find the carousel.
The island was so small
It felt almost like a backyard,
With very few places to know
And hardly anywhere to go.

A great charm of a carousel is its slow circular motion,
A pattern consistent with the designer's notion.
Generally speaking, moving in circles is considered a drawback
As you seem to take a few steps forwards and then a few back,
And you never seem to get anywhere.
Most destinations are in the forward direction,
And any movement that prevents forward motion causes a delay,
Even if you travel in the right circles and know your way,
But about that matter children were mostly unaware
And the great joy of the ride meant they did not care.

So, the idea of a mechanical ride that takes you round and round
Seems counterintuitive and very unsound,
But nonetheless many rides follow the same gyration,
As being propelled in the air brings exhilaration,
And about the rotation people rarely did complain,
For moving in an orbit does not in any way your pleasure constrain.
The carousel is a good example of a ride to nowhere
That can be enjoyed over and over again—
You experience motion with musical accompaniment, feeling free of care.

Of course, if the speed of the ride were too slow
That could easily ruin the show,
And if asked to pay for such a ride, most people would usually say no.
Slow motion creates monotony and brings in one's mind a herd of sheep
And the rider on counting them could easily fall asleep
And become enveloped in a dream about a hillside pasture so very steep
And, for the shepherd, those wooly creatures would be hard to keep
As they could wander off in any direction, and logic would tell you
That if you found one, you'd lose another. There was no telling where it would hide,
Especially in twilight (for they often moved without a peep).
Immersed in daydreams that wandered far and wide,
The customer, eyes fixed on the approaching tide,
Would not come back for another ride.

The carousel was a familiar destination during my childhood;
For a summer evening outing, it was an option that was good.
It was a good compromise as the distance to Broad Channel
Was not so far as Rockaway Beach and its large amusement park,
And often you could arrive there well before dark
On a route that was direct and easy to travel,
A place where the stress of the day could at once unravel.

I would say that at age five,
The carousel was a grand attraction
Which would always bring great satisfaction
To kids, who'd go like bees to a hive,
A place where fun and gaiety would thrive.

I remember the carousel mostly in the hours of twilight,
When the sky over the bay was tinged scarlet by the setting sun—
It was an early evening trip there that started the fun.
The channel was quiet and the hubbub of the carousel filled the air,
Heard just before the carousel came into sight.
The place had very few visitors and was never overly congested,
As in amusement parks most people were much more interested.
People would come with the family, as an individual, or in a pair.
Somehow, that jewel of the island escaped the notice of people crossing the bay

On their way to the island of Rockaway,
But the carousel definitely had a group of devotees
Who destiny chose to bring to that place.
They seemed to fit together like the bay and the breeze.

The merry-go-round, very special for a younger or older kid,
Was like a cookie jar without a lid.
It had an assortment of stationary and moving wooden horses
Modelled after the swift-as-the-wind steeds at the racecourses,
Who would gallop along its edge as the music would play
In early evening and well into the night.
For children the merry-go-round was a joyous sight,
And if the place closed at three AM many would have chosen to stay,
Such was the degree of derived satisfaction.
The ride was illuminated by lights
Of many colors, adding to its attraction.
Whirling around, they looked like flying kites.
Some would blink on and off and others would remain lit;
You could see them from where you would sit.

The moving horses were on the outer platform perimeter.
From there, you could grasp just about anything in reach,
And what you could get was dependent on the platform's diameter
And the location of the object you were trying to grasp,
But it was no secret to confide
That it was particularly advantageous to grasp a ring
While the rotating platform was on the glide.
However, that certainly was not an easy thing;
A carousel worker, a man on a ladder, would load the ring holder
With metal rings and if you reached out and grasped for a ring of gold
You could redeem it for a free ride and gain a story to be told.
Grasping the ring was easy
And there was rarely a kid that got queasy,
And it became easier as you got older
As your strategies for reaching out became bolder,
But getting a gold ring was a challenge;
Your chances were best on a galloping steed at the head of the phalange

Coney Island

As the gold rings were in very short supply
And the odds were against you
(As any calculation would verify as true),
And most people would say it was pie in the sky,
But nonetheless you always would try,
And if you ever snatched one,
Great joy from within would spring
And prompt even the most sedate rider to rise up and sing,
A feeling that certainly added to the fun.

Family Ambassadors of Goodwill

Isaac and Sarah Balsam, family pioneers, emigrated from Austria-Hungary.
In about the year 1900, they settled in Lower Woodhaven near Jamaica Bay,
Predominantly farm country, a remote and thinly settled area in the day.
They came in search of opportunity and to build a family
And their principal business plan was to establish a dairy.

Isaac and Sarah had six children, born in the Balsam homestead near the farm
On Lower Woodhaven's southern border.
Maxwell, Paul, my father, Morris, Rose, Leon, and Nathan, in that order.
For the children, the farm country held great charm.

In the early days, all of the children helped on the farm;
Rose would help Sarah with household chores,
And with all the sand outside, that meant sweeping the floors
And also raising the chickens in the fourth house upstairs.
It was said that raising chickens is not as easy as it looks.
Rose was a sister to five brothers and she looked out for them every day
And keep them out of the way of harm.
She would help serve their meals and assist with every day cares
And in the business, she was the keeper of the books.

Growing up in the first two decades of the twentieth century,
All of the children attended public schools,
Where they learned reading, writing, and arithmetic rules,
With attention to detail that was far from cursory
Also taught were civic responsibilities and the principles of citizenship.
It was the time of proper spelling, grammar and penmanship
Practiced and developed with writing drills
And there was an emphasis on craft skills
And adding long lists of numbers by hand,
Which must have seemed like counting grains of sand.
Special attention was given to the orderly working of long division
And for remainders, you were taught to make a provision.
Rose excelled in all disciplines as a student,
Emphasizing study routines that were indeed prudent,

And she was multilingual and excelled at writing.
Approaching ideas with an enthusiasm that was exciting,
She became a cultured person with a fine education,
As to learning standards she was a very high-reacher.
She became a language teacher,
A diligent worker of great dedication,
And to the family, she was always a great inspiration.

She fell in love with Philip Isaacs, a young naval officer,
Who was born and grew up in the Lower East Side.
He was a friendly and trustworthy person in whom you could confide,
The type of person who could easily tell how good and bad offers were.
He studied law and became an attorney, and they married and lived in Manhattan
In the center of the city, on Park Avenue, in a district of silk and satin.
Philip Isaacs was the personification of love, polish, and demeanor,
An all-around person in settings opulent or lean,
With great warmth and charisma which would brighten any scene.
He served as the attorney for Balsam Farm in the early days.
He was a great advocate for the family as he knew their ways,
A person who prudence always would heed,
A person who would look out for the family's needs.

He had a fascinating combination of seriousness and mirth,
A New York City person by birth,
Which you could recognize in many ways:
He was always formally dressed, a business prerequisite in those days,
With a white shirt and tie and highly polished shoes,
As if he was about to march in a wedding processional.
A perceptive person who always recognized cues,
He was a very engaging person and always very professional.
He was a person in whom method, demeanor, and warmth coalesced,
With a diplomatic approach free of condescension.
The nature of his profession you could have easily guessed:
He worked for a law firm that specialized in bonds and pensions,
And you could understand why he was successful at first glance.
He had sophistication with a remarkably steady stance.
But it was the warmth and charm he projected that created a bond,

And clients valued his advice and of him were very fond.
He excelled at examining conflicts in all dimensions
And clearly was an expert at resolving dissensions.

Growing up in Ozone Park, I would often see Aunt Rose and Uncle Phil,
An engaging couple with family involvement that had love at its core.
He loved thoroughbred horseracing and knew all the racing lore—
For racing aficionados, Ozone Park was like a candy store
Where you could buy more than enough candies your pockets to fill.
It was renowned for the racetracks its residents did construct,
And our neighborhood had a very successful racetrack, Aqueduct.
In earlier times, there were other tracks for the lover of the racing horse
Located in the neighborhood like Centerville and Union Course.

Every year a ritual occurred that involved a happy exchange.
It was a family initiative that someone had to arrange
And the person to perform the task was Uncle Phil,
With the goal to supplement a child's allowance and fortify the till,
So before he could accomplish what he was appointed to do,
You would see his smiling face as he approached to greet you,
Always with an outstretched hand for a formal handshake,
A gentlemanly greeting for kindness's sake.
At least once a year, he concealed something in his right hand,
A custom applauded by nieces and nephews as grand,
And in the handshake you received a ten-dollar bill—
That was what I call a gift of love, and for each family child a great thrill—
The after-birthday calling card of Uncle Phil.
And that bill bears the image of Alexander Hamilton, another New York attorney,
A brilliant financial legal scholar who wrote prodigiously with ink and quill,
The father of our monetary system since the beginning of our nation's journey.

And occasionally that experience would be revisited in a dream
(For many pleasant occasions recur when telegraphed by moonbeam)
In great detail, and I'd remember his largesse and conviviality,
The dream had only a slight deviation from reality:
On a table were several crisp uncirculated specimens, each a ten-dollar bill,
And from the center of their green surfaces smiled the face of Uncle Phil.

At the turn of the century it took about a day to travel to Manhattan and back.
It was still the era of the horse and carriage,
And from the cabin you could hear the horse's hooves go clikety-clack,
And the scant comforts of that ride you could easily disparage.
On the outskirts of the city since the 1800s, Woodhaven soon became more accessible
As the desire for rapid transit became irrepressible,
And with easier transportation there was much to gain,
For children in the area could now take the train.

In the neighborhood of Ozone Park in the 1940s,
I frequented two favorite destinations
To which travel didn't require much patience.
In the north, Forest Park and in the south, Balsam Farm,
And to those places I would regularly make a variety of sorties
Whether the weather was cold or warm,
But I found Manhattan to be a complex and very distant place,
One of considerable interest and with many a saving grace.

Manhattan was a world unto itself, indeed,
A world of culture, education, entertainment, and adventures galore,
And certainly it had all of that and more.
It sparkled with creations of a unique breed.
The place was a great sensation,
Like none other in the whole nation.
The myth of comic-book Gotham couldn't shine the shoes of that location,
For the splendors of the city were legion,
Well known across the whole region:
Architecture, art, urban design, the park, the rivers, stylish retail,
And great in appearance (even at night, when the lights did prevail).
Great dynamism around that place swirled,
A class act so unique it was the light of the world.
The skyscrapers were an absolutely awesome creation
And for local folks and tourists from the rest of the nation
Their uniqueness was indeed an inspiration.
At about age eight, I would occasionally go with my father to Downtown,
And the office of Uncle Phil was a popular destination,
A site that was a common place for many a visitation,

Though to me the purpose of the visits was unknown.
It was in the Empire State Building, and any visit there was a great thrill
And an experience that great respect for architecture would instill.
Facing Lower Manhattan, the firm's offices were on a floor at a very high location.
Looking out the window, you felt that you were mostly in the sky;
You could almost reach out and touch the skyscrapers nearby,
And in the distance great views opened before you in the light of day—
You could see the Hudson River, the East River, and below the Battery, Upper Bay.

From that high perspective, you could see very narrow streets appear below,
With tiny yellow taxis streaming south or north
And other vehicles lost in the yellow wave moving back and forth.
It was very difficult to see any people from that height—
They were too small and inconspicuous to come into sight.
They were like miniatures that moved along like creatures in a herd,
So small were they, tinier than a bird,
And from that level you had grand views of the city and felt great inspiration,
And in that wonderful building you came to an important realization
About the great promise of the Roaring Twenties to the entire nation,
Whose fulfillment had been delayed by the Great Depression—
It was as if the hard times made an important concession
That the promise would be kept sooner or later,
And likely in a way that was even greater.
It was made by innovators, who in creative pursuits were great believers
And who came from a generation of spectacular achievers,
And indeed history remembered that it had a vow to fulfill.
It was delivered by a generation with an indomitable will
And the grandeur of that impressive monument to Art Deco style,
An architectural pattern of substance which would last more than a while,
An epic work of modern architecture rising into the sky,
It is hard to grasp how it was built so high,
Grander than any palace on Earth, a towering symbol of modernity,
Rising up near Herald Square, a major epicenter of the city.

Since the early 1900s and even before,
Manhattan was known for the theater, the stage, and the stage door.
There was often spectacular dancing and a wonderful musical score

In the early days featuring vaudevillians,
Which appealed to millions:
A mixture of acts featuring the singer of a ditty
And the comic, with one-liners which were very witty,
But vaudeville was on the way out when the talking movies arrived.
It was difficult to compete with the action on the silver screen
And wherever you sat everything could be seen,
But there were vestiges of vaudeville which survived
In the Paramount Theater at the epicenter of Broadway,
Which had a double program: live entertainment and a full-length movie together,
A new entertainment combination on the Great White Way
And a strong enticement in rainy or sunny weather.

At various times I made excursions to that place
To attend a matinee performance on a trip like a race,
As to latecomers the program's schedule offered no grace.
I took the A train all the way to 42nd Street
And like a whirlwind that express train accomplished its feat,
Bringing me to 42nd Street Station in the west,
And from there it was easy to find the Paramount, a bustling location
At the corner of 43rd Street and Broadway, very close to the subway station,
Where I would often meet one of my cousins, also an invited guest.
One aspect of the experience in particular comes to mind:
We were instructed to go to the theater's back door
(And it was certainly easy to find the way)
And to the attendant "Two for Isaacs" to say,
Whereupon he escorted us to our seats,
Usually quite near the front and at the end of an aisle,
To enjoy live performances and its treats,
Which would usually start in a very short while.
Grateful we were to our sponsor, Uncle Phil,
Our benefactor behind the scenes
For treating us in such wonderful style
And doing all the work of an ambassador of goodwill,
But on that day he was nowhere to be seen.
On the stage, pride and joy of New York City,
The performances were of great diversity:

Comedians, dancing ladies and gentlemen, and singers were standard fare.
The performances would divert your attention from any mundane care
Without the props and costumes in which the previous generation found great thrill.
You could say that they were the last vestiges of vaudeville.
The neighborhood movie emporium, the Crossbay Movie Theater,
Was built in 1925, and designed for orchestra and vaudeville presentation
To take advantage of vaudeville's popularity, part of the plan of the business creator,
But that did not last, as talking movies became a great novelty and a great sensation.
They were very popular and lengthy, and at the Paramount, the movies were first-rate.
They would come there early but to the neighborhood late.
In those days, movies were shown for a long time before a new one came—
There was no need to check the newspaper as the film was mostly the same.

In the late 1940s, the couple would spend the summer in Long Beach.
They stayed at the Jackson Hotel on the boardwalk by the beach
And their nieces and nephews would visit them to enjoy summer at the shore.
With the kids around, there were always surprises galore;
It was a favored place to vacation and escape the city summer heat
Although, unfortunately, I was too young to participate.
There were many stories that my cousins would relate
About their experience visiting their aunt and uncle on a summer vacation treat.

Phil loved the ocean and would travel around the world,
Over which the flags of many nations unfurled.
He would arrange for long voyages across the seas
Mostly in the mid- to late-1960s,
Past one continent and then another, to remote islands with eucalyptus and palm
Far away from Manhattan and from Balsam Farm.
He was alert to all the deals offered by a travel agent he knew,
And he and Rose would spend much of the year at sea,
Sometimes as much as six months, and there was always plenty to do.
On occasion they would circumnavigate the globe on a voyage of discovery.
The ship was a home away from home, a position the fine boat earned,
And Phil and Rose would report on their adventures as soon as they returned.

I recall seeing them off on one of their trips
On the West Side, at a point of disembarkation of transatlantic ships.

Coney Island

They invited the family on board the ship, which was docked at a wharf
On the Hudson River at about 57th Street,
And in that place the whole family did meet.
It was a very cold day in January and I recall wearing a coat and a scarf.
It was fun to wish them well as they began their voyage,
And their great ocean-faring vessel on the Hudson was certainly no mirage,
At a place so close to where the explorer's ship appeared after a long voyage at sea
And the occasion was a joy for them and the entire family.

From the Balsam Farm to Steeplechase Park

Part I: The Balsam Farm

As a child growing up in Ozone Park during the 1940s,
I felt that I had two homes, which feels odd to say—
One was in Upper Woodhaven of yore
On 94th Street near 101st Avenue, formerly called Broadway,
Near the Woodhaven Presbyterian Church and the penny candy store,
And the other was south of Liberty Avenue, the Balsam homestead,
Adjacent to Balsam Farm in Lower Woodhaven and close to Jamaica Bay
Where my father and his brothers and sister were born and bred.

I always thought of the farm as the eighth world wonder
For several reasons, particularly its futuristic automation,
And it was also home, a place about which you would certainly be fonder.
But I would have to say that Tilyou's place was a rival for that designation,
For it was also one of a kind and a very innovative creation
That to its many devotees was a great sensation.
The mere thought of the place was beckoning
So, according to my reckoning,
After considering the matter and starting to ponder,
I decided that the A train should be awarded the title of ninth wonder
And the automobile the tenth,
And Steeplechase the eleventh.

I came to know Steeplechase during the late 1940s
And indeed, there are many stories that could be told.
Adventures did not occur on occasional sorties,
And so I feel that it's important to provide additional background
In which multiple associations can certainly be found
To give the reader a better understanding of how things did unfold.

The Balsam Farm was my second home, I can proudly say,
A consideration that was more than just a feeling of family loyalty;
It was because I spent most weekends in the Balsam homestead near the bay

And as the sun descended on Friday evening, approaching was royalty:
The coming of the Sabbath Queen, a symbol of holiday grace,
Whose benevolent spirit filled the city-country place,
Permeating the Balsam Homestead in every cranny and nook.
Stories about my experiences there could easily fill a book.

From Friday night at sundown the Sabbath was observed
Until Saturday evening, when the first three stars could be seen.
It was a longtime tradition from which the family path never swerved.
In the nighttime sky, as darkness descended upon the scene
And quiet reigned on the farm on the holy day,
It was a day of rest and no business was conducted,
A custom so ingrained that no family member had to be instructed.
It was my grandfather Isaac Balsam's practice, such was his way,
That the Sabbath Day be reserved for prayer and celebration,
A very important element in the family history narration,
And no work was done on that day, a longtime tradition,
Following a pattern of the generation of the great transition.

In the synagogue Congregation of the Sons of Jacob he constructed,
Friday night and Saturday services were conducted
With congregants from the neighborhood, each of a similar tradition and like mind,
Where at the turn of the century on the first Rosh Hashana, the Shofar was sounded
In the small synagogue that he had founded,
Emphasizing a message that we learned from the early pioneers of our nation,
Who sought a new life with the unconditional right of religious determination.
Opportunity and religious freedom are so often intertwined
And indeed, in the family's life they were closely combined.

The Balsam Farm had kept religion in mind seven days a week
As it was a dairy farm whose product was kosher milk,
With a radiant white luster and a taste as smooth as silk,
One that Jews from Eastern Europe would particularly seek.
It was a product that was born early in the Jewish diaspora, affirmed by the sages,
A dietary tradition that was in place in Central Europe for many ages
As religious Jews were not permitted to drink milk from farms
That raised hogs or sold non-kosher products for consumption,

And when there was any doubt, not kosher was the prevailing presumption.
But the milk was popular irrespective of religious preference;
In New York's neighborhoods and in every geographic section,
Growing children required it to develop strong legs and arms.

In the quiet of the Sabbath day,
On the farm, family traditions held sway.
My brother Joel and I spent the Sabbath day on the farm,
A semi-rustic place in the city with considerable charm,
With our Aunt Mollie, Uncle Morris, and cousins Jack, Martin, and Sara Sue,
A family experience with no genuine substitute I knew.

For a city child on the farm experiencing Sabbath celebrations,
They had a uniqueness compared with children's experiences in other generations.
It was a joy, but much of that was related to the farm,
Which from the home seemed to be only the distance of an outstretched arm.
You could walk across Pitkin Avenue and visit the cows
Amid the sounds of the cats' meows.
There was an informality about the animals that was inviting—
There was never a bad time to visit and it was always exciting.

You could throw the football around in the cow pasture
And you could put on a padded glove and catch a baseball in the side yard
Or juggle three pairs of socks in the family room
(If three pink bouncing balls were unavailable)
To produce a feeling of exhilaration that was unassailable
And if one got away it might spell disaster or doom
But that was no cause for pessimism or gloom—
To retrieve it you would launch a dedicated chase
And when you touched it there'd be a smile on your face.
Yes, all that was possible in that happy scene
Where the skies were bright blue and the trees they were green.
Upon remembering the Sabbath on the farm
I note that the Sabbath is a spiritual kingdom traditionally
Whose reigning monarch is the Sabbath Queen,
Who embraces the holiday scene with her grace unconditionally.
She is the guardian of the Lord's holy day,

Who descends from heaven on Friday at the last daylight
And departs the earthly sphere on Saturday night.

And if the Sabbath Queen ever had a sister, I would say
Mollie Balsam was her name,
So devoted was she to preparing for the holy day—
And in her person, selflessness and modesty were one and the same,
For she'd put aside personal interest in favor of her family's satisfaction,
Always stalwart in faith and resolute in action
And very devoted to her religious traditions.
Even when facing trying conditions,
She welcomed guests in the tradition of each matriarch
To the Balsam homestead in Ozone Park.

At the festive meal on the Sabbath day
Two honored guests often were present:
Aunt Rose and Uncle Phil.
Sharing time with the family was their way
And spending time with them was always a great thrill:
They brought to the table love and conviviality, a great sensation
Adding much to the festivity and making it pleasant.
For them it was like reliving the experiences of the earlier generation
When, with six boisterous children, the home was humming,
A destination to which family and friends were often coming.
I could tell that Aunt Rose was very attached to the Balsam homestead
And the family farm, where she was born and bred.

The Sabbath was never uninteresting or limiting for the children,
Even though it presented many unique religious restrictions and conditions.
According to tradition it was time spent in the Lord's dominion
And at the Balsam homestead there was a unanimity of opinion
In favor of keeping up religious traditions
That had been honored since antiquity
And had continued for all of history.

At the conclusion of the Sabbath on Saturday night
There is a celebration in honor of the Sabbath Queen

As she departs from the earthly scene,
A farewell before her trip back to her abode in heaven,
Her path illuminated by the moon and stars so bright.
The party is called a *Milave Malka*, or "Escorting the Queen."
And for about a year after I reached the age of eleven,
I experienced the weekly celebration in Tilyou's spectacular kingdom.

Part II: Steeplechase Park

It was Coney Island in its glory,
A subject of many a fabled story,
And my visits were always on Saturday night.
The nighttime parks were always a delight,
And few flaws could be recognized beneath the gleaming lights
And we children would have adventure in our sights.

From afar you could see Wonder Wheel illuminated by a profusion of lights,
The wheel rotating slowly, always seeming to reach for new heights,
And Parachute Jump rose out of the darkness of night,
Facing the silent bay glistening 'neath the moon shining bright.

In the distance you could see the Steeplechase Park sign,
Giving no hint of its treasures, its grand adventure equine.
It rose more than one hundred feet high
As if it were trying to touch the sky.
At the top of a towering iron grillwork, as high as you could get,
Was a large smiling visage like that of a jovial wooden marionette.
The features were exaggerated on the figure's happy face,
Its famous grin the signature of the place,
Brimming with mirth and indeed very wide
Its smile stretched from side to side,
And an appealing gleam lit up its eyes,
Illuminating even the skies.
It was a sign of the fun characteristic of Steeplechase,
Signaling the joy of the park, even after dark,
That even straight-laced fun disparagers could not constrain.
I entered Steeplechase from Bowery Street through the gateway to Tilyou's domain.

You could say this about the world of Geo. C. Tilyou:
It was a place that would certainly thrill you.
When the effects of all the flying, rocking, twirling, spinning, and falling left you,
You often felt unstable on your feet and occasionally dizzy too,
And sometimes would even wonder whether you were still you.

And before recommending to anyone the domain of Tilyou, a master of motion,
You had to consider one very simple notion:
It was not a place for a person sensitive to the moving state,
For its ill effects you could not underrate:
Queasiness was one, for which there was no medicinal potion
And that feeling you would certainly hate,
But there were alternatives, needless to say:
Send him to the boardwalk, the beach, or the bay.

On entering Steeplechase from the Bowery Street side
I would walk through the rotating barrel without much difficulty,
For I'd quickly become accustomed to the tube so slow and wide.
Once you understood the rhythm of the barrel, that rotating peculiarity,
You could move through it without losing your balance and falling,
And you came to wonder how any tightrope walker found his calling.

There were four favorite places
Which were like magnets for me,
Consistently bringing adventure and glee
Inside the park and outside:
First was the Steeplechase ride,
Where it was off to the races.
There was illumination from the rest of the park
And beyond, all you saw was inscrutable dark.
Yes, that was definitely the feel
And within it was the steeplechase apparatus was made of steel
So, up to the hills
And down to the dales
Your trusty steed sails
On a ride that gave you chills.
We'd not go to the country on a summer day

Or to riding trails,
But rather to the other place
Named Steeplechase
With sand and sun
And a whole lot of fun,
Where children would bring shovels and pails
And winding in the air were tracks in man-made courses
Along which you would ride wooden horses,
Steeds with names not known
Which had no minds of their own
And could not even wag their tails;
But they could glide up and down the rails
And there was only forward motion
And a quiet without commotion,
With no list to either side
On tracks that were not very wide.

On the horse in the starting gate, you would look at the course in its starkness
And then your trusty steed would plunge forward into the darkness.
You held on to its neck as an added safety measure
So you could finish the race in good style, which was a genuine pleasure.
The sound of a bugle on your ears would grate,
And a moment later a bell rang at the starting gate.

That ride had a definite ring of reality
In a setting that was remarkable for its conviviality,
And often you did not know who actually won the race—
Such was the experience of Steeplechase,
A very big attraction, the glory of the place.

Another attraction I particularly enjoyed was very close to the Steeplechase ride:
Just behind was a gigantic wooden slide.
It was made of highly polished wood and was very wide,
And you could descend, taking a very long glide;
You felt the excitement of the fall and there were turns as well.
The ride was exhilarating and spectacular, truth to tell
I recall sliding without shoes to avoid excess friction,

And there was plenty of room for a sideways spin
While avoiding a crash and a fall on your chin.
It was considered too dangerous to wear rubber-soled shoes
And a warning sign alerted you to that interdiction,
Though after one bad experience that alert became old news.

Third on my list of favorites were the bumper cars.
Indoors, it did not matter what the weather was under the stars.
A ride that had a very interesting history, generally getting riders' raves.
The initial version of that ride was called Witching Waves
And was located outside Steeplechase Park near the Bowery.
The open-air ride was difficult to enjoy in weather that was showery—
People would ride alone or in a pair,
And the cars had seats like those of an oversized high-arm chair,
As if from someone's living room they were on loan,
And they followed an uncertain route (they did not move on their own).
The person in the car holding the steering wheel did not actually drive it—
It veered randomly and there was no telling what it would hit.
There was no ability to accelerate or to turn,
But the ride was too much fun to spurn.

It was the metal flooring underneath that moved in waves
Like a banner waving in the breeze.
The ride was indeed an experience that did please
And its unpredictability garnered raves.
It was the undulation of the undersurface that propelled them forward,
And you depended on chance to prevent anything untoward.
Even that primitive system of moving the cars
Kept the people happy enough in the park and out of local bars.

The earliest bumper cars reminded me of the earliest motorcars:
Very basic and primitive in many ways, not sturdy,
Generally reliable for fair-weather day trips but not after six-thirty.
You have to come up with something before you reach for the stars,
Not surprising as the first cars weighed only about one thousand pounds
And were quite noisy, making a variety of loud sounds.
Without sturdy suspension, the jostled rider of the ride was much more aware,

But the adventure of the trip tended to make people not care
And the tires were almost as thin as bicycle tires of today.
On gravel roads, they kicked up a lot of sand on the way.

Bumper cars that I drove in the late 1940s and early 1950s were in their prime,
If I had to rate that ride, I would clearly rank it among best at the time.
There was no gasoline motor to churn,
And with electric power, you could accelerate and turn.
They had the mobility that the driver craves
With a power system that energy certainly saves,
And you had greater control of those two-seater cars.
Compared with those in the Witching Waves,
They indeed were the brightest stars.

You were almost guaranteed to get bumped,
But you were protected from getting lumped
As there was plenty of padding around the vehicle and an oversized bumper,
But your car could easily be thrown off by a lady in slacks and a jumper.
So you would drive around the indoor track as best you could,
And there were traffic rules to be honored, if you would.

On occasion there was civility with normal flow of traffic,
But then things would unravel and people blurted expressions graphic.
The ride was in a fairly dark and closed space indoors,
And often lighting was limited to a low overhead light here and there.
With less light on the scene, drivers had to beware!
And there was noise rivalling the waves on the shores,
Increasing the challenge of navigating the oval track as best you could.
One side of the track was separated from the other
By an elevated median where a traffic monitor often stood.
Frequently you would see two mischievous kids, a seven-year-old and his brother,
And you could easily predict that the duo were up to no good.

The drivers of the cars were of all sorts.
Of particular concern was the unruly child who with danger cavorts!
Many were very unused to the experience
And that was a recipe for a bump, it had all the ingredients,

And others were quite experienced but very boisterous.
In addition, there were drivers who were mischievous:
Looking for trouble, they seemed bent on bumping others,
Even cars occupied by children with fathers and mothers.
What is the typical response of those in a bumper car
Who have only recently entered the car and not gone very far
But have lost their way and were about to be bumped?
If you were asked this question you should not be stumped:
The answer surprisingly is robust laughter,
And that often lingered long thereafter.
That frivolous reaction notwithstanding, a plan was needed to get out of the way
And what that plan should be in any given instance, you could never really say.

In that ride many uncertainties did arise,
Bringing the important elements of excitement and surprise.
It was not possible to look in more than one direction at a time,
And some drivers were less proficient and were not in their prime.
Avoidance did not depend on driver capability
And getting bumped was of high probability,
A principle that in all drivers was easy to inculcate.
If your car hit a complicated tie-up, it was a challenge to extricate,
Especially in the setting of reckless drivers,
Some of whom were expert connivers.
Also, if you were involved in a multi-car tie-up
And got to facing traffic's direction,
Another car could send you into a pathway of deflection,
And there was no telling where you would wind up.

Outside the park, I liked the Cyclone on the corner,
Like the plum pulled from the pie by Little Jack Horner.
On Surf Avenue and West 10th Street
Stood the island's earliest roller coaster,
And you could sing the praises of that ride without being a boaster.
A great place for the adventurous to meet,
It was constructed in 1927 once its plans were complete.
From my perspective, being an early model was an advantage and treat:
A less steep and more manageable ride but no less of a feat,

And I felt that its compact design your enjoyment did not diminish.
It was plenty fast and many riders would confide
That it was a very exciting ride,
An adventure from start to finish.
Getting on and off was very easy,
Though the ride was over very fast
And it left many people queasy
In calm or windy weather—
So my thinking was always to leave that ride for last
And sometimes to skip it altogether.

There were certainly many other rides and fun places
That I favored less but occasionally did try—
After all, with new adventures one should never be shy.
Most of those rides gave you the feeling of being off to the races.
The caterpillar was one of those,
A rapidly moving coaster from open to close,
A ride advertised on a Coney Island street poster
That at one point in the ride was covered completely
By a green canvas cover that cast you in the dark.
While you were moving on the coaster,
You could see nothing in the park
But that cover was soon removed and tucked away neatly.

At the close of the Saturday night entertainment bash
In that wonderful and entertaining milieu,
You could definitely proclaim without being rash,
"Thank you, Mr. Tilyou!
Your rides are an inspiration!"
And Steeplechase Park, a favored destination
With people so happy to be inside
For more than one generation,
And the architects of the favorite park and ride
Also deserve our thanks and hearty cheers,
For their role as Coney Island design pioneers
Of amusement parks: to the nation, a great source of pride.

On the Boardwalk

The Coney Island boardwalk is a twentieth-century invention,
One that has many functions and attracts much attention.
It is a raised platform several feet above ground level
With a wooden slat flooring, providing a surface without a bevel
Over a steel and concrete foundation,
Giving the structure its elevation,
An innovation inspired by the sea-view attraction,
For gazing at the sea gives people great satisfaction.
The boardwalk is actually the street that borders the beach,
And its location brings that place easily in reach.

The boardwalk is mostly a pedestrian walkway
With a full view of the beach and the bay.
Small shops and concessions are located on the other side.
In the early days, from open storefronts vendors plied,
And from the boardwalk a person can descend stairs
Either to the beach or the adjacent street.
Summer visitors come alone, in groups, or in pairs.
It is a convivial place for people to meet:
You can perambulate in any direction or sit on benches,
And you are caught in summer fitful clenches.
The passersby watch the goings-on at the shore
And the sights observed are never a bore.

In a ceremony that met with much glee,
The boardwalk was officially opened on May fifteenth, 1923.
Extending to Brighton Beach from Sea Gate,
A distance of about two and a half miles.
The walk along that elevated platform people did highly rate,
Bringing to their faces lots of smiles.
With benches, guard rails, and street lights along the beach side,
The walkway was very long and fairly wide,
And along it you would see people dressed in a variety of styles.
There were entrances to amusement parks from the boardwalk in the early days,

But only a few of those remain today as the visitors developed new ways.
You could say that the boardwalk was a child of public transportation.
It was not long after the subway arrived that the boardwalk was built.
In the early days, it gave people a third choice, a sand-free place of elevated station
Where the sea breezes on a summer day would ensure that you would not wilt.
You could head for the amusement park or the beach or the boardwalk—
Each a possibility and either a choice with which you could be complacent—
And a decision in favor of one or another could be made rapidly without much talk,
Leading to the prospect of the joy of adventure nascent.

To illustrate the popularity of the boardwalk:
In the 1920s and the 1940s you could see people milling about.
It was a place where you would never be isolated, within or without,
As you always were in a crowd and there was plenty of talk
About baseball games and current motion picture rages.
The boardwalk would be teeming with people of all ages;
Caught up in the crowd's wave, no person stood still,
And those individuals for stores were fillers of the till.
Occasionally, there was standing room only;
It was a place where you never were lonely.

In the open air, the noise was never very loud,
Whether the sky was clear or filled with cloud.
In the 1920s, people on the boardwalk were formally dressed,
With a high sense of fashion that generation was greatly blessed:
Women wore dresses while men dressed in suits with ties and hats.
And ladies often carried parasols, walking along on those wooden slats;
It was a grand sight, one that could make you proud.

The boardwalk can withstand strong ocean winds and heavy storm showers
And overall it has great weight-bearing powers.
There was no fear of a broken fate;
You could drive a car on that structure, not just perhaps,
And there was no concern about structural collapse
As the boardwalk was built on a very solid foundation
And matched the strength of just about any structure in the nation.

With less strong construction, collapse would have been a very real concern,
As a wooden platform would not be strong enough to carry the crowd's weight,
And there would be hesitation at every turn,
An experience people would surely want to spurn.
In contrast, the Coney Island boardwalk's structural integrity you could highly rate.

In its heyday, Coney Island was the number-one amusement park in the country.
The island was also a popular destination because of the beach.
Mostly working-class people would take the subway, largely common folk
Enjoying the spontaneity of the unstructured setting and a good joke,
Which public transportation easily brought within reach.
The experiences there were diverse and sundry,
And generally speaking the beachgoers did not drink four o'clock tea,
Not on weekdays or on Saturday or Sunday—
There were too many adventures waiting to bring afternoon glee.

As time moved on, there were changes in demographic patterns
With the ascendancy of middle-class satins.
Populations moved to Long Island in the east,
And the automobile as a popular means of transportation lead to greater mobility.
That conveyance was a spectacular wonder of transportation to say the least,
As you could easily get to faraway places in a car.
Roads to the shores gave day visitors direct access with greater facility,
And other beaches spread to the east, competing with the Brooklyn sandbar,
And the automobile brought people to other destinations, taking business away
From Coney Island, which was so dependent on the elevated subway train
And to a certain extent the place lost much of its luster and became plain.
Many factors caused Coney Island to wane;
Simply stated, it was another day with another way.

In the Roaring Twenties, people were fond of the walkway by the sea.
On the beach, there was relief from modern-life complexity.
It was a magnet for a happy crowd,
Whose members were very proud.
It was also a place for fraternization,
With mingling and socialization.

You could develop friendships and fraternity
And people could relax and talk.
It also provided extraordinary views of the bay and the shore,
But the mobile individual could definitely see more.
For a full complement of the sights, most people would walk,
But some wanted to enjoy all that but at walking would balk;
For them, a carriage powered by a human was just next door;
It had many of the features of a rickshaw,
The man-drawn carriage on the boardwalk.
Food concessionaires offered Coney Island fare,
And dissatisfaction with that was very rare.
Also very popular with every guest
(For whom a day of pleasant adventures was the central quest)
Who came to enjoy the day and set aside any care
Was a souvenir, an island ware
That could be bought in a souvenir store
Or in other boardwalk gift shops galore.

There was also the studio of a photographer
Who in the world of images served as a biographer.
On the boardwalk his studio was considered a fixture
As there was a strong demand for taking your picture.
There were few cameras in the early days,
So the function was left to professional enterprise,
With results that were often a great surprise.
He added various props to give the scene an authentic mixture,
Which could present the person in different settings and in various ways,
A method that was appealing for many and considered very sound.
And one day the place was visited by a junior stenographer,
Who found props showing country scenes in the background:
A complete set with meadows and barns and a haystack
To be featured at the subject's back.
An image of the sun was added to round out the picture
And in the studio, the city girl thought that a country setting would be fun.
A picture would serve as a souvenir that would not be outdone.
The subject would stand on a platform which was very sturdy,
And the photographer would say, "Watch the birdie."

Then came a bright light that left the subject unshaken
And in a flash, a picture was taken.

On the boardwalk, adding variety to the scene, were purveyors and vendors
Looking for people who were unabashed spenders.

A man played a hurdy gurdy,
Presenting a daytime show with a dancing monkey,
For whom the boardwalk became a stage in a play that was not very wordy.
The monkey was dressed in a red coat, a box-shaped cap,
And a wide leather belt with a shiny copper buckle.
He held a cane during the show,
And took it every place he would go,
And the skit was not tied to any specific rubric.
At intervals there was accompanying music
Adding a thematic enhancement acoustic:
He struck the cane against the wooden stage with a tap, tap, tap!
His antics would make the audience smile and chuckle
And their response was clap, clap, clap!
And no matter how prodigious the athletic displays
(Which indeed appeared effortless and easy),
There was little danger that his energy would sap,
As by nature climbing and jumping were his customary ways,
A routine that would make the average person queasy.
A lady sitting on a bench had her eyes glued to the show;
She said there was little danger of her taking a nap,
As there was too much excitement going on and she was in the know.
Thankfully, there was little danger of the monkey jumping on to her lap
As his master had attached a long leash to his belt
With an exterior of leather and an interior of felt.

The boardwalk was a place to enjoy the sea breezes without the sand,
For the views of the island surroundings were indeed grand.
Many people had exactly that preference;
They'd walk the boardwalk and be very sociable.
It was a casual place, so there was no need for deference,
And there was an overflow of people in the limited space.

Alan Balsam

A good view of the beach was never guaranteed or even negotiable,
But whenever you walked on the boardwalk you always found a happy face
As people were there for recreation and of their own volition,
And appeared to be enjoying themselves in that informal social coalition.
It did not matter who you were or where you came from, if that came up in talk,
You were always a welcome member of the crowd on the boardwalk.

At Coney Island Beach

For family outings of adventure, fun, and relaxation,
Coney Island is an ever-popular destination.
Its beach is the principal attraction,
And the sea and sun are a source of great satisfaction.
The seashore provides respite from the city heat,
And for that purpose it is hard to beat.

Several aspects of the island's development are worthy of mention,
General facts that help with overall comprehension,
Providing a better understanding of its diverse stories
These can be summarized under the following categories:
Access, transportation, population growth, beach, bathing wear and style
And each of these developed over a very long while.

Access to the beach from the mainland
Is essential for visitors as the beach is on an island.
Starting in the 1800s the landscape was devoid of human sensitivities:
An isolated, rugged sandbar subject only to nature's proclivities.
But soon development of transportation access provided,
And also to be considered is how the growth of the mainland was decided.
Large numbers of people came from nearby, sustaining business activities.

Access to Coney Island improved in 1829,
And for future development it was a welcome first sign.
They opened a route leading to the shore and the bay,
Creating for vacationers a holiday destination to seek.
A bridge was built from the mainland over Coney Island Creek
By the Gravesend and Coney Island Road and Bridge Company of that day.
It was a basic structure that could not take heavy loads,
And trips to the island during the next two decades were over carriage roads.

There was also a sea route to the island from the battery port
Located near the settlers' early fort.
The views from that steamship were great,
But the trip would take a few hours even when conditions were best.

In 1847, the ferry brought you to Norton's Point, terminus of the island in the west.
The company also built Coney Island House, the first hotel on the island in Sea Gate.

Then came railroad tracks to the island and so started their envelopment,
Signaling a new milestone and starting a brisk pattern of development.
In the 1860s, the excursion rail lines arrived:
The Coney Island & Brooklyn Railroad streetcar line
Allowed for access of which the island had hitherto been deprived.
In 1875 came Prospect Park and the Coney Island railroad line,
A happy event that would allow the island to shine,
Sending out a welcome to families and to ladies and gents
And bringing Brooklyn people to the island for thirty-five cents,
Generating revenue and enabling business owners to pay their rents.

But even with the railroad station in the middle of the island,
There was mostly inactivity in the byland.
The annual number of visitors was small
And at the time, it seemed that the order for change was indeed very tall.

The 1870s brought development in the east,
Creating new summer recreation opportunities
With the development of the Brighton Beach and Manhattan Beach communities,
Upscale resorts which were more appealing than Coney Island, to say the least,
Which was in disarray and had fallen on hard times.
The area was not well kept and had been overtaken by street gangs
Who stalked the neighborhoods, caught in urban blight's fangs.
Politicians decried the lawlessness but there was little action with their rants;
It was in an atmosphere of corruption that all the trouble did brew,
And in such conditions, tourists to the area were few.
So, beach and business activity on the island was scant—
It was a time when the horse stood behind the cart
Waiting for a new catalyst to bring a fresh start.

As access to the island was consistently improving,
The engine of development started moving
And there were better facilities for the beachgoer.
Rapid transit sped up things that were once considerably slower;

Coney Island

Before, conveyance to that destination had been so slow
That it almost seemed you were not moving, it was hard to know.
After several hours travelling there'd not be much day left to seek,
And in those days the drivers of the carriages were definitely not meek
And under no circumstances about their driving would they take any cheek.
The place was therefore not for short clips
And that essentially ruled out day trips.
So for a visit to the beach, better plan a three-day stay or, better yet, a week,
A great way to dispel boredom and gloom:
You could reserve a beachfront hotel room,
And for many families such routines were annual traditions.
But you can readily understand that under such conditions,
The number of summer visitors to the place was small,
As limited access and high cost put a damper on any beach plan
For the immediate family or aunts and uncles and cousins, the entire clan,
So people visited the area only occasionally, or not at all—
But things started to change in a dramatic way
In the days of the horse-drawn shay
With the arrival of the railroad train and the first subway line.

It is generally said that people should be dressed for all occasions,
And that aphorism applies to beachgoers as well.
Bathing wear is an important matter, truth to tell,
And has a long history of change for people of all persuasions.
In the mid-1800s, ladies' bathing suits of full length
Were made of heavy cotton, a fabric with extra strength—
Women could wear them on the beach or on the deck of a schooner
And as a general rule they would meet all the standards of Amelia Bloomer.
Men wore two-piece suits and tank tops over bathing shorts,
Conducive to swimming and other beach-related sports,
While women wore paletot coats with ballooning Turkish pants of ankle length
Or else bathing suits made of flannel with great material strength.
But as it absorbed water, a bathing outfit's weight decreased its buoyancy,
Making swimming very difficult in the calm, much less the rough sea.

At the turn of the nineteenth century, until a few decades later,
Pants were replaced by shorts extending below the knee

And long stockings were added, a better combination for the sea
And one that to active adults did cater.
Laced-up bathing slippers were also favored as an accoutrement,
For proper fashion was an important element prescribed by comportment.
The women's suits were so elaborate that there was no hope they would dry,
Even with the summer sun shining in a cloudless sky,
Bringing to the seashore the heat of midday,
The glare of its rays glistening in the bay.

In the days of oversized bathing wear
The island was very difficult to reach,
And there were few people on the beach.
If there were deviations from the accepted style,
There was little possibility of a concern to share
As the closest person might be at the distance of a mile.
You understood why so few businesses could take hold,
As the season was shortened by the coming autumn cold
And there was not enough activity about which to care.

But things were about to change and there were two major factors
That would wake the sleepy island to the buzzing of building contractors:
First, the arrival of new immigrants from eastern and southern Europe;
And second, the inexpensive rapid transit that would soon make its way to the place.
The population of the city swelled about three and a half fold,
And opportunity was knocking at the door as there was much to be sold.
In the near future, your foot would be on the boardwalk or in a wooden horse's stirrup
On the fabulous racecourse suspended in the air, Tilyou's Steeplechase.

Coney Island over the years gained easier access through public transportation.
The railroads opened and brought you to the island's only station—
However, a major advance occurred in about 1917, the year
A great change in the type of transportation was soon to appear,
When the city expanded transportation with two private vendors' binds
And the new Brooklyn Rapid Transit Company under dual contracts
Acquired the Brighton, Culver, Sea Beach, and West End railroad lines,
An acquisition that promised to increase your island contacts.
The subway ran overhead as an elevated line and to a new terminal it did wind,

Coney Island

The Coney Island Stillwell Avenue Station.
Under the beaming island sun that new station did shine,
Creating in public transportation a great sensation.

When the subway system took over the railroad lines,
Rides cost nickels and it took another two decades before it cost dimes.
The beach and its amusement parks became known as the Nickel Empire,
An entertainment center with diverse delights of which you would rarely tire.
The inexpensive subway trip was the inspiration for the name's genesis,
And it would bring you to the Stillwell Avenue station and nearby premises.
The ease and low cost of transportation attracted crowds to the place,
And for just about anybody who came it was a welcome change of pace.
Weekend attendance was almost standing room only;
It was an empire in which you could never feel lonely.
What the exits to the elevated station looked like you could only guess,
But any speculation into the unknown tends to be useless,
As getting close to them was exceedingly difficult no matter how you tried.
On the beach you were lucky if you could find space to spread a towel,
And on the boardwalk you'd be swept along with the human tide;
You had to protect your feet as one person's misstep could make you howl.

In the 1920s there were business possibilities in the city
And hard-working people did not hesitate to explore the nitty-gritty
As that might have led to a missed opportunity,
Which would have been a great pity.
They sought what was genuine and rejected what was phony
And recreation was not far away near at the island of Coney,
Where the acts were so much more than the proverbial dog and pony.
As a place for a date you could bring your honey
And, as it was inexpensive, you'd only spend little money.
Whether the day was cloudy or sunny,
It was busy during the entire summer season,
And on seeing the place you could understand the reason.
The parks were open at night and attracted many visitors at that time
But the beaches were desolate and shimmered in the moon glow.
In the sky's canopy, the stars were so still that you wished they would move to and fro.

But as night ended its stay,
Quiet ruled over the bay,
And as the sun began its ascent, the first glimmer of daylight visited the island.
The sandy beaches stood in stark contrast to the mainland;
Not a soul could be seen for miles along the silent shore,
And the gentle morning tide reawakened and came to the fore.
Sea creatures were active, creeping along diverse paths
And the birds were starting to visit after their departure at nightfall:
They seemed to be drawn to the place by a siren's call.
Where those birds spent the night is totally unclear,
But then they circled the sands in broad swathes.
An eerie quietude reigned as the dawn did appear.

All that changed as morning set in,
Before the arrival of the daytime din
And beachgoers who appeared on the beach scene.
That moment in time was for action and there was nothing to be said—
Blankets were spread over the sand,
Umbrellas were planted firmly to provide shade from the sun,
Multicolored, some with white, red, and green,
And as the sun moved more directly overhead,
People kept coming, an endless human tide in search of relaxation and fun,
Taking refuge from the heat of the city and the drudgery of the day,
Away from the burden of work and goals not always within reach
Into the lap of informality, a carefree sunny beach,
Where the sand could be felt by bare feet and so could the water of the bay,
And new people of similar mind and spirit you could meet.
It all added up to an experience that was a great treat,
Though the summer day had turned on its heat.
The people came as if borne on the wind's wings
To that one small space, the land where the sanderling sings,
Like birds returning from their winter home,
A faraway place from which they roam.
The beach was filled like a glass to the very brim,
And one glance told you that just a few more people, even very trim,
Would serve as a wedge,
Pushing the rest on to the boardwalk or to the water's edge.

It cost a nickel to go to the beach by subway
And so many people did just that.
If you missed one train there was no need to scowl
As another was on its way.
You could wear a bathing suit under your clothes and a sun hat,
And bring along a towel,
And you'd be on your way.
The ride on the train was exciting, too,
As the elevated line had a view.
You could sense you were getting close to the island
As you felt the sea breeze even though you could not see the sand.

With excellent conditions for bathing just about every summer day,
Coney Island's beach faces Lower Bay.
If you are standing on the beach and you close your eyes and wonder
Whether you are on the bay or the Atlantic Ocean,
You can't necessarily tell; nothing's told by the water's motion,
And doing some sort of test would not be a blunder,
So if you put on a wide-brim beach hat
You would soon get an answer like a blast of thunder.
It would not matter whether you stood or sat;
On the bay, hats always stay on,
And on the ocean they generally blow off.
If they're not chased down, they could soon be gone.
At those observations it is hard to scoff,
So doing the hat test is valuable,
Though its precise value is incalculable.
Of course, based on only that evaluation
And using only that calculation,
You can't always decide where you are, it would be hard to say,
Particularly based on only a few minutes' stay.

At the beach, people would come alone or with family and friends
Who received the message that the siren of summer sends.
It was a place that answered recreation's call,
Providing a great day's outing to be enjoyed by all.

You could find opportunities to embrace the sand,
Which had a changing shape and was warm and yielding,
Moving in any direction with the push of a hand
Or at the behest of a child a shovel wielding.
Shifting from one place to another in patterns that had no limit,
It was forgiving, unlike the hard surfaces of the city street,
And it was accepting of sandals or bare feet.
It could serve as a pillow piled up with a towel over it
Or could shield your feet from the sun's rays
Even on the brightest of summer days.

The Coney Island sands had an orange tint,
The surface of which had a very distinct glint
Characteristic of the Brooklyn sandbar along the bay
And much more noticeable at the end of the day,
Unlike the sands on the Atlantic beaches to the north:
Jones Beach, Long Beach, and Rockaway,
Blown by the wind but always pristine white
With the ocean waves that were rough and gushed forth.
Raising the prospect of fun and adventure and not merely a casual hint
In those places, the glaring summer sun was so bright
That a glance in its direction would make you squint.

In the open air, even with so many people on the shore
And with the ocean breezes and the breaking waves, there was little to be heard;
Sometimes, oddly enough, not even a word would come to the fore.
People were often idling about and there was little commotion;
For newcomers it was, "Pass me the suntan lotion
And then that magazine from home."
Waves washed ashore in a burst of foam,
Echoing like a musical refrain,
And these could be heard above all else, and the distant hum of an oncoming train.
Conversations of people were muffled by the sand and the breezes of the sea,
And the shouting and laughter of children at play
With unbridled enthusiasm and glee,
Was limited to a dull roar.

Coney Island

As the clouds rolled in over the bay
Beachgoers showed no concern about an imminent downpour.

The music was played by the island's unheralded four-piece band,
Featuring the beachgoers, the wind, the waves, and the sand.
The beach was so crowded you did not see a single bird, an exceptional instance,
From the sight of all the people they kept their distance,
And a person had to wrestle with an important choice,
Which had a persistent inquiring voice:
Where and which way to go?
To buy an ice cream cone from a boardwalk emporium
To satisfy gustatory pleasures of the sensorium,
Or to repair to the beach on the waters of the bay,
Which were generally calm and without much undertow?
The best choice was difficult to know.
Another possibility, the amusement parks, would keep you busy for the rest of the day.
Whatever was the actual choice, daylight waned as day moved out of sight,
And at that time there was utter desolation on the beach in the starkness of night,
But that transitory absence of light would yield to the sunrise on the way.

A Tribute to Coney Island

O, ancient barrier island
Adrift off the mainland
Where land meets the sea,
Exposed to the ocean's merciless fury,
Whose early chronicles are mostly unknown history.

In more recent days
Change has come in many ways
To the formerly chaotic and windswept island,
A great credit to the human hand
That brought order to the domain of the sand.

Here, facing the challenges of the ages,
As described in the history book's pages,
Live a people of resolute will yearning to be free
Who chose to confront adversity,
Always taking a stand, not deciding to flee.

Island rich in history,
Bearing many an important legacy
And many an unfolding story
Of love and glory.

O, island of fate's gyrations,
Bringing joy to many generations,
Welcoming to its shores people from many nations,
Helping them build new lives in a land of opportunity,
Gathering different types and creating a single community.

Island of achievement throughout the ages,
A place of great accomplishment;
Isolated sandbar changed by development,
Better fortified to withstand the sea's rages.

Coney Island

Many dreams of earlier generations
Have been realized over the course of time,
And some have clearly been great sensations
While others have not yet reached their prime.
Some unfulfilled dreams remain, looking for opportunities to glean;
Those dreams are like birds of spring, flying above an ever-changing scene,
Leaving home before winter in search of warmer climes
And thankfully returning in spring to find better times.

www.ingramcontent.com/pod-product-compliance
Lightning Source LLC
Chambersburg PA
CBHW081153090426
42736CB00017B/3299